WORD AS IMAGE

"I lodge my feelings here"
Seal impression from *Wu Rangzhi Yinpu* (No. 47)

WORD AS IMAGE
The Art of Chinese Seal Engraving

Jason C. Kuo

CHINA HOUSE GALLERY
CHINA INSTITUTE IN AMERICA
New York City
1992

Distributed by
The University of Washington Press, Seattle and London

Cover illustration: Details from *Handscroll of seal impressions*.
Ink on paper. Chien Lu Collection
(no. 52, front cover: DLT; back cover, vertically from
right to left: AIQ, CK, BJR).

© 1992 China Institute in America. All rights reserved
Library of Congress Catalog Card Number: 92-73978

General Editor and Coordinator: J. May Lee
Consulting Editors: Ann Lucke, Marilyn Wong Gleysteen
Book Design by Peter Lukic
Printed and bound in Hong Kong

China House Gallery, New York City
Exhibition: October 24-December 12, 1992

China Institute in America is a nonpolitical, nonpartisan,
bicultural organization founded in 1926 to promote better
understanding between the American and Chinese peoples
and to assist Chinese in the United States.

ISBN 0-295-97253-X

CONTENTS

Lenders to the Exhibition **7**
Message from the President **8**
Foreword **9**
Acknowledgements **11**
Chronology **13**
Word as Image: The Art of Chinese Seal Engraving **15**
Color Plates **63**
Catalogue of the Exhibition **73**
Reference List **90**
List of Chinese Characters **97**

LENDERS TO THE EXHIBITION

The Art Institute of Chicago

The Brooklyn Museum

Chien Lu Collection

Robert Hatfield Ellsworth

Field Museum of Natural History, Chicago

Professor and Mrs. Hans H. Frankel

Gest Oriental Library and East Asian Collections, Princeton University, New Jersey

Guanhai Lou Collection

The Guennol Collection

Dr. Sesin Jong

The Metropolitan Museum of Art, New York

Dr. Paul Singer

F. Randall and Judith G. Smith

Wang Fang-yu and Sum Wai Wang

Yi Lei Wang

Wan-go H. C. and Virginia Weng

Dr. and Mrs. Clyde Wu

Yale University Art Gallery, New Haven

MESSAGE FROM THE PRESIDENT

China Institute in America is proud to present this exhibition, "Word as Image: The Art of Chinese Seal Engraving." Through the display of seals, impressions, calligraphy, archaic objects, and limited-edition seal books, this exhibition explores the relationship between seal-engraving and the art of calligraphy in the development of the Chinese script. It also advances the mission of China Institute by promoting an appreciation and understanding of a significant component of Chinese art, history, and culture. "Word as Image" will intrigue audiences from all walks of life, from scholars and connoisseurs to school children.

This exhibition would not have been possible without the support and assistance of many individuals, foundations, and corporations. We are especially grateful to The Henry Luce Foundation and the Starr Foundation for their continuing generosity toward, and involvement in, our work. In addition, I wish to thank the Gallery Committee, chaired by Marie-Hélène Weill and Millie Chan, for their indefatigable efforts to rally support for this exhibition, and the Art Committee, chaired by Annette Juliano, for reviewing and selecting this exhibition. We are grateful also to the School of Chinese Studies for coordinating the lectures and symposium related to this exhibition.

There is one individual we wish to thank who is not with us to witness the opening of the "Word as Image" exhibition. Myron S. Falk, Jr.—Johnny to his friends—was a longtime friend and supporter, without whom there would be no China House Gallery. He was instrumental in its establishment and, as a member of our Art Committee, helped to guide the Gallery through more than twenty-five years of programming. The Institute has organized a memorial lecture series in Johnny's name, as a tribute to a beloved patron of Chinese art and of China Institute. Thank you, Pauline Falk, for your support and assistance in this endeavor.

Above all, I extend my warmest appreciation to our Gallery Director, J. May Lee who, with this exhibition, bids farewell to China Institute. Under May's guidance, the Gallery has experienced a renewed vitality and vision. May will be greatly missed by the staff, the Board of Trustees, and all who have worked with her these past several years. We say "goodbye" to May, but wish her and her new family every happiness.

Charles P. Wang
President

FOREWORD

The idea to do an exhibition of Chinese seal engravings was an extremely compelling one. It challenged China Institute in an area that it already excelled—the presentation and interpretation of little-known aspects of Chinese culture to the American public. Often overlooked in general surveys of Asian art, seal engraving is an important and multi-faceted subject once thought to be comprehensible only to a handful of Chinese connoisseurs. To the Western art historian, these small, red seal impressions, ubiquitous on paintings and calligraphy, represented a key to authenticating works of art. This exhibition leaves such a complex issue to future studies. Instead, seal engraving is presented here as an art form directly related to calligraphy. Each impression bears the golden aura of antiquity in its use of archaic scripts. At the same time, a well-carved seal distinguishes the engraver and the user as learned and aesthetically sensitive individuals.

Calligraphy and seal books have also been included in this exhibition to add greater depth to our understanding of seal engraving. Clearly, the seal engraver must also be a calligrapher; both face the same problem of interpreting an ancient script style in a modern context. On the other hand, the practice of collecting seal impressions into books, or *yinpu,* demonstrates the importance of seals as an independent art form. A seal can be appreciated for its own sake, not merely as an adjunct to a painting or a piece of calligraphy. Seal books are also witnesses to the Chinese habit of collecting. Although this exhibition borrows exclusively from museums and collections in the United States, it is recognized that the serious collecting of seals began in China and that many fine collections of seals, such as these of the Shanghai Museum and the National Palace Museum, have already been published in Asia. We are only making a small, initial step in the same direction.

China Institute is grateful to its guest curator, Dr. Jason C. Kuo, Associate Professor of Art History and Archaeology of the University of Maryland. His expertise in the history of Chinese painting and calligraphy and his personal knowledge of seal engraving has been brought together in the writing of this scholarly catalogue. We join him in thanking the lenders to this exhibition and in acknowledging the pioneering effort of the Yale University Art Gallery in their exhibition, "The World Within a Square Inch: The Art of Chinese Seal Carving." In exhibiting contemporary seal carvers, Yale curator Qianshen Bai, reminds us that this art form is a continuing tradition. We are also indebted to the visionaries in the Art Committee, particularly James C. Y. Watt and Annette Juliano, who saw that this was an appropriate and timely subject for our Gallery.

The organization of an exhibition and publication of a catalogue from conception to fruition is a long and complex process. Along the way we have enlisted the help of many generous and talented people. Collectors and institutions have not only lent us their artwork, but have also given us countless hours of assistance with such chores as research, translations, photography, and cataloguing. I would especially like to thank Maxwell Hearn, Marilyn Wong Gleysteen, Sören Edgren, and Professor Wang Fangyu for their personal assistance in this project.

Our gratitude goes also to the artistic consultants who worked long and patient hours to transform raw material into final, polished reality. The numerous photographs, rubbings, and seal impressions presented a special challenge for our designer, Peter Lukic, to blend all the parts into an attractive, coherent whole. Perhaps even more challenging was the job of Carl Nardiello, our installation designer, who had to combine a diverse selection of objects ranging greatly in size and shape. We are indebted to LeMar Terry, who continues to advise us in technical matters and assist in the lighting of our exhibitions.

We are fortunate at China Institute to have a dedicated and multi-talented staff. Heidi Schulman kept track of all the loans and doubled as staff photographer, while Hai Weilan double-checked the romanization and compiled the list of Chinese characters. In addition, we are grateful to our friends and volunteers, Lymeng Ly, Don Kim, and Tim Barrett, who assisted in the less glamorous but necessary tasks involved in putting together a catalogue. An advance word of thanks goes to the volunteers who act as docents and gallery attendants during the exhibition and, in particular, to Florence Landau who keeps track of the storage and sales of each new publication of the gallery.

China Institute is most of all grateful to its Sponsors and Patrons listed at the end of this catalogue and its Gallery Committee, chaired by Marie-Hélène Weill and Millie Chan. Their enthusiastic support of China House Gallery sustains our programs and breathes vitality into the cultural life of our community.

Jung May Lee
Director
China House Gallery

ACKNOWLEDGMENTS

The exhibition and the publication of the accompanying catalogue have been made possible through the support and generosity of many people and institutions. First of all, I would like to thank all the lenders who have most generously shared their collections.

I would also like to express my sincere gratitude to the following individuals in particular:

To Stephen Addiss, Professor of Art History, The Kress Foundation Department of Art History, University of Kansas, for his encouragement.

To Milo C. Beach, Director, Freer Gallery of Art and Arthur M. Sackler Gallery, Smithsonian Institution, Washington, D. C. for his generous support.

To Chiang Chao-shen, formerly Curator of Calligraphy and Painting and Deputy Director, National Palace Museum, Taipei, for introducing me to the art of seal-engraving many years ago.

To Richard Edwards, Professor Emeritus of the History of Art, University of Michigan, for his advice and unstinting help, and for giving me the opportunity to study the seals on the works of art from the National Palace Museum, Taipei.

To Doug Farquhar, Professor and Chairman, Department of Art History and Archaeology, University of Maryland at College Park, for his unceasing encouragement and support.

To Shen C. Y. Fu, Senior Curator of Chinese Art, Freer Gallery of Art and Arthur M. Sackler Gallery, Smithsonian Institution, Washington, D. C., for his constant guidance in the connoisseurship of Chinese calligraphy and painting.

To Lily Kecskes, Head Librarian, Freer Gallery of Art and Arthur M. Sackler Gallery, Washington, D. C., for her bibliographical assistance.

To Thomas Lawton, Senior Research Scholar and former Director, Freer Gallery of Art and Arthur M. Sackler Gallery, Smithsonian Institution, Washington, D. C., for his advice on early Chinese art.

To Steven V. Owyoung, Curator of Asian Arts, The St. Louis Art Museum, for his enthusiastic support from the very beginning of this project.

To Naomi B. Pascal, Editor-in-Chief, University of Washington Press, for her encouragement and support.

To Jerome Silbergeld, Director of the School of Art and Professor of Art History, University of Washington, Seattle, for his strong support.

To Jenny So, Associate Curator of Chinese Art, Freer Gallery of Art and Arthur M. Sackler Gallery, Smithsonian Institution, Washington, D. C., for her advice on bronze inscriptions.

To Wang Fang-yu for sharing his knowledge of seal-engraving.

To James C. Y. Watt, Brooke Russell Astor Senior Curator, Department of Asian Art, The Metropolitan Museum of Art, for his advice.

At the University of Heidelberg, Germany: Lothar Ledderose, Professor of Art History; Lothar Wagner, Sinologisches Seminar.

At The Metropolitan Museum of Art: Maxwell Hearn, Associate Curator of Chinese Art; Judith Smith, Administrator, Department of Asian Art; Caron Smith, Assistant to the Director.

At the University of Maryland at College Park: Robert Griffith, Dean, College of Arts and Humanities; Donna Hamilton, Associate Dean, College of Arts and Humanities; Marcus Franda, Director, Office of International Affairs; Courtney Shaw, Head, Art Library; Fan Kuang-yao, Head, East Asian Collection; and all faculty and staff members of the Department of Art History and Archaeology.

At Princeton University: Wen C. Fong, Edwards Sanford Professor of Art and Archaeology and Special Consultant for Far Eastern Affairs at The Metropolitan Museum of Art; J. Sören Edgren, Director, International Union Catalog of Chinese Rare Books Project; Martin Heijdra, Chinese Bibliographer, Gest Oriental Library and East Asian Collections.

At Yale University: Richard Barnhart, Professor of History of Art and former Chairman of the Department of History of Art; Mary Gardner Neill, The Henry J. Heinz II Director, Yale University Art Gallery; Colin Mackenzie, Associate Curator of Asian Art, Yale University Art Gallery; Bai Qianshen, graduate student, for sharing their pioneering exhibition "The World Within a Square Inch: The Art of Chinese Seal Carving."

At China Institute in America: Charles Pei Wang, President, and Annette Juliano, Chair of The Art

Committee, for organizing and supporting the exhibition. Without the patience, resourcefulness, and cooperation of J. May Lee, Director of China House Gallery, and her assistants Heidi Schulman and Hai Weilan, the completion of this project would have been impossible. Ann Lucke and Marilyn Wong Gleysteen edited the manuscript and made invaluable suggestions.

I would like to dedicate this publication to Edie and Eileen who, during the time I worked on this project, often competed with my word processor for my attention but not my affection.

Jason C. Kuo

CHRONOLOGY

Neolithic	c. 7000-1600 BC	Song Dynasty	960-1279
Xia Dynasty	c. 1850-1600 BC	Northern Song	960-1127
Shang	c. 1600-1027 BC	Southern Song	1127-1279
		Jin Dynasty	1115-1234
Zhou	1027-256 BC	Yuan Dynasty	1280-1368
Western Zhou	1027-771 BC	Ming Dynasty	1368-1644
Eastern Zhou	771-256 BC	Hongwu	1368-1398
Qin Dynasty	221-206 BC	Jianwen	1399-1402
		Yongle	1403-1424
Han Dynasty	206 BC - AD 220	Xuande	1426-1435
Western Han	206 BC - AD 9	Zhentong	1436-1449
Xin Dynasty	9-23	Jingtai	1450-1457
Eastern Han	25-220	Tianshun	1458-1464
Three Kingdoms	221-265	Chenghua	1465-1487
		Hongzhi	1488-1505
Six Dynasties (Southern Dynasties)		Zhengde	1506-1521
Western Jin	265-317	Jiajing	1522-1566
Eastern Jin	317-420	Longqing	1567-1572
Liu Song	420-479	Wanli	1573-1619
Southern Qi	479-502	Tianqi	1621-1627
Liang	502-557	Chongzhen	1628-1644
Chen	557-589	Qing Dynasty	1644-1912
Northern Dynasties:		Shunzhi	1644-1661
Northern Wei	386-534	Kangxi	1662-1722
Eastern Wei	534-550	Yongzheng	1723-1735
Western Wei	535-557	Qianlong	1736-1795
Northern Qi	550-577	Jiaqing	1796-1820
Northern Zhou	557-581	Daoguang	1821-1850
Sui Dynasty	581-618	Xianfeng	1851-1861
Tang Dynasty	618-906	Tongzhi	1862-1874
		Guangxu	1875-1908
Five Dynasties	907-960	Xuantong	1909-1912
Liao Dynasty	907-1125	Republic	1912-

NOTE TO THE READER

Chinese is romanized in the *pinyin* system throughout the text and bibliography except for the names of Chinese authors writing in Western languages. Place names have been modernized to the *pinyin* system only for locations within the People's Republic of China. Chinese terms cited in Western language titles remain in their original cited form and have not been converted to the *pinyin* system. The characters for the romanized Chinese used in the text and catalogue sections are found in a separate section at the back of the catalogue.

Exhibition objects in the text are followed by their catalogue number in parentheses. Impressions of the seals in the exhibition are illustrated in the catalogue section along with rubbings and additional views.

WORD AS IMAGE:
THE ART OF CHINESE SEAL ENGRAVING

Jason C. Kuo

Although a seal is small,
no longer than a finger, and no larger than two square inches,
it contains development and structure and, in its sweep and profundity,
can be as satisfactory as a fine work of literary art.[1]

Verba volant, scripta manant
(The spoken word passes, what is written remains).[2]

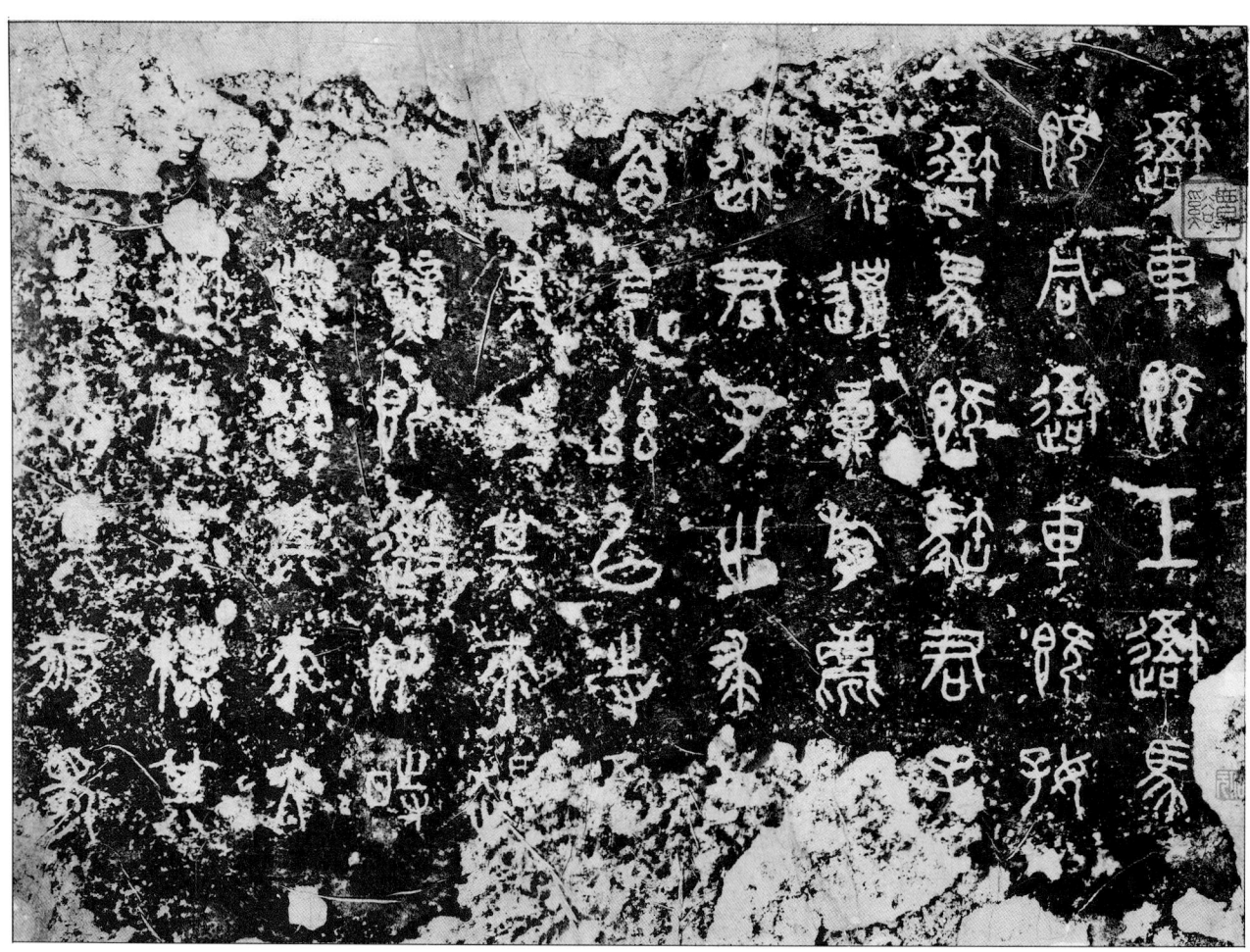

Pl. 1, (No. 1). **Rubbing of Inscriptions from the Ten Stone Drums (8-3rd c. B.C.)** Ming dynasty (1368-1644). Section of a handscroll. The Metropolitan Museum of Art, New York; Promised Gift of Wan-go H.C. and Virginia Weng, 1989

In Chinese civilization seals were symbols used to indicate ownership, to authenticate documents, and to establish political or religious authority from as early as the second millennium B.C. By the 16th century, seals were also regarded as aesthetic objects by the elite; even so, their function as symbols of ownership and authority never completely disappeared. In traditional Chinese painting and calligraphy, seals are used to produce the small vermilion marks that are affixed onto the artwork by the artist, his friends, or by collectors and connoisseurs. Seals, or "chops" as they are commonly called by Westerners, record either a name or a commendatory phrase that has been engraved in reverse onto a stone or some other hard material.

Even today, a person in China and other parts of East Asia cannot cash a check at a bank without presenting a seal of his or her personal name, and a piece of calligraphy and painting seems incomplete without an impression of the artist's seal.[3] Despite their small size, seals are significant objects in the cultural history of China, for several important reasons.

First of all, seal engraving can be considered a special form of the art of Chinese calligraphy. Most seals are engraved with a type of script widely used on ancient monuments of ritual, power, ideology, and authority from the second millennium to the third century B.C. The script type has come to be known as seal script, or *zhuanshu*. Chinese calligraphy, with its beauty of linear rhythm, has been regarded as one of the quintessential elements of Chinese pictorial art. As the English critic Roger Fry once stated, "A [Chinese] painting was always conceived as the record of a rhythmic gesture. It was the graph of a dance executed by the hand. This predominance of linear rhythm is felt in all Chinese decoration and even in sculpture."[4] To this, calligraphy or seal engraving are no exceptions.

Second, as a medium for reproducing images and texts, seals are related to printing, one of the most celebrated Chinese contributions to civilization. Beginning in the Six Dynasties period (A.D. 265-589), seals together with the use of rubbings were an important factor in the development of printing.[5] In fact, the same word, *yin*, is still used today for both printing and seals.

Finally, ever since the fourteenth century, seal engraving has been regarded as an important aspect of the literati's cultivated pursuits. A large body of critical and historical literature concerned with seal engraving has been written and preserved. A recent dictionary of calligraphy and seal engraving lists over one thousand titles on the subject.[6] In the West, a few doctoral dissertations and books have recently been written on the art of seal engraving;[7] however, apart from a brief discussion by Robert van Gulik many years ago, there has been very little, if any, opportunity for the general public to see, learn, and enjoy the fascinating art of Chinese seal engraving.[8]

In a culture in which the educated elite have had little regard for any pursuit with connotations of physical labor and in which the names of architects and sculptors have been rarely mentioned, Chinese seal engraving has been highly regarded because of its affinity to the art of calligraphy and out of respect for the written word.

SOURCES OF THE ART OF SEAL ENGRAVING

Cultural Significance of Ancient Scripts

In order to understand the art of Chinese seal engraving, it is necessary to consider not only the scripts on the seals themselves but also those found on ancient monuments, for seal engravers since the fourteenth century turned constantly to these models for inspiration. As a special form of Chinese calligraphy, seal engraving can best be appreciated through apprehending the nature of calligraphy as an art form and the historical and cultural significance of the seal script in its various permutations and transformations.

The origins of writing in China have long been equated with the origins of Chinese culture. In the commentaries to the *Yijing*, or *The Book of Changes* (ca. 6th-3rd century B.C.), it is stated:

> When in early antiquity Paoxi ruled the world, he looked upward and contemplated the images in the heavens; he looked downward and contemplated the patterns on earth. He contemplated the markings of birds and beasts and the adaptations to the regions. He proceeded directly from himself and indirectly from objects. Thus he invented the eight trigrams in order to enter into connection with the virtues of the light of the gods and to regulate the conditions of all beings.[9]

This mythical birth of the trigrams have traditionally been regarded by the Chinese as the origin of their written language. Archaeological evidence indicates that true Chinese writing probably began in the late third millennium B.C. The ancient myth cited above clearly demonstrates the Chinese conception of writing as the embodiment of power, authority, culture, and antiquity.[10] It also explains in part why Chinese calligraphy in general and seal engraving in particular later evolved into high art.

According to Cai Yong (A.D. 133-192), one of the earliest writers on Chinese calligraphy, the great seal script, or *dazhuan*, of the Shang and Zhou dynasties had a divine quality:

> Of the six types of calligraphy,
> The seal script is so marvelous that it is divinelike.
> It is like the tortoise shell's pattern,
> Or like the scales of a dragon;
> Sinuous, with a tail-like ending,
> Long wings and a short body;
> The neck sticking out, the wings wide spread,
> Flying out to the clouds.

And the small seal script, or *xiaozhuan*, developed in the third century B.C., was:

> Like the tortoise shell's pattern,
> Like needles in row;
> Like a comb's teeth, dragon's scales,
> Extending like the beards of cereal grass;
> Like curled up caterpillars crawling all over,
> As though separated, as though united;
> Like the gossamer threads of deep-water algae,
> Solid by their strong roots.[11]

Undoubtedly because of the association of writing with the divine and the power of creation, some Daoists believed that seals carved with writing could expel evil spirits. For example, Ge Hong (ca. 283-343) noted in his *Baopuzi* (ca. 300):

> The ancients who went up to the mountains wore a "yue zhang" seal of the yellow god, four inches in breadth and having a hundred and twenty characters. With the seal, they made impressions on sealing clay that they placed around the spot where they had chosen to stay, one hundred steps long on each of the four sides. Tigers and wolves did not dare to go inside this barrier. If, while traveling, the ancients saw a tiger's fresh footprint and impressed the seal there in the same direction in which the beast had moved, they made the tiger proceed in the same direction; but if they impressed the seal in a contrary direction, the tiger turned back. As the result of having these seals with them in the mountains, the ancients were not afraid of tigers and wolves. Moreover, they could make bloodthirsty, evil gods of the hills and streams or temples powerless by placing seal impressions on sealing clay along the path—if there were such evil gods capable of causing unhappiness or bad luck.[12]

Calligraphy, which has often been regarded as superior to painting as a fine art, also preceded painting in losing its predominantly didactic purpose. The rise of purely aesthetic attitudes toward calligraphy took place during the Eastern Han dynasty (25-220).[13] As early as the Western Han dynasty (206 B.C.-A.D. 9), the philosopher Yang Xiong (53 B.C.-A.D. 18) spoke of calligraphy as the "picture of the mind."[14] Today, the self-expressive power of calligraphy can still be found in the popular saying "To see a man's calligraphy is to see his face."

Seal Script Before the Han Dynasty

The earliest systematic script type to develop in China was oracle-bone script (*jiaguwen*), which appears on oracle bones that were used for divination during the late Shang dynasty (middle of the second millennium B.C.). The characters were first written with a brush and then engraved with sharp tools into hard, unyielding bones or tortoise shells. They tend to have rather sharp edges and generally a static configuration. Oracle bones were rediscovered around 1900 near Anyang, Henan Province, and research into these bones has confirmed the historicity of the Shang dynasty. Although oracle-bone script was never used on seals during the Shang period, many twentieth-century artists have successfully adapted this script in their work, thereby enriching the repertoire of the art of Chinese calligraphy and seal engraving.

Another script type developed in the Shang dynasty and used widely in the Zhou dynasty (ca. 1050-256 B.C.) was a style of writing used in inscriptions cast with bronze vessels (*jinwen*). Characters were usually first incised into the soft clay molds from which bronze vessels were cast, and the inscription transferred to the clay core so that it appears as intaglio on the inside surface of the finished vessel (Pl. 2, Fig. 1). The characters in these bronze inscriptions tend to have rounded corners rather than the sharp corners of the earlier oracle-bone script and they also tend to combine coarse and fine strokes, usually without sharp endings. However, the characters still lack a standardized size or form.[15] The rediscovery and study of bronze inscriptions began in the Northern Song dynasty (960-1127) and was revived in the later part of the Qing dynasty (1644-1912). During the early twentieth century and particularly in the past forty years, scholars have intensively investigated these inscriptions in conjunction with controlled and systematic archaeological excavations throughout China. Regional inscription styles have been defined and their chronologies have been established. Since the late Qing dynasty, inscriptions on bronze have become a great source of inspiration for seal engravers as they sought to broaden their knowledge of earlier and less codified models than the small seal script.

There are two subtypes of seal script or *zhuanshu*.

Pl. 2 (Fig. 1a). **Ritual Food Container (Yu) with Lid.** Western Zhou dynasty, 11th-10th c. B.C. Bronze. Arthur M. Sackler Gallery, Smithsonian Institution, Washington, D.C. (S1975.5)
(Fig. 1b, c). **Rubbings of inscriptions.** Inside the lid (b) and bottom (c) of the *Yu* are identical inscriptions which read, "The Marquis of Yan made this *yu* for travelling."

Great seal script, or *dazhuan*, refers to the inscriptions found on bronze ritual vessels of the late Shang and Zhou dynasties; small seal script, or *xiaozhuan*, refers to the script type codified by Qin Shihuangdi, the first emperor of the Qin dynasty (221-206 B.C.), in the early third century B.C. This new unified writing style was promulgated between 219 and 211 B.C. in seven imperial edicts inscribed on stelae or mountainsides to praise the achievements of Qin Shihuangdi's administration and to legitimatize his reign. Rubbings of these monumental inscriptions have been a source of inspiration for many later calligraphers and seal engravers. Unlike the earlier great seal script, small seal script has even strokes and rounded corners, and each character is vertically rectangular in shape.[16]

Broadly defined, seal script comprises almost all script forms developed from the beginning of the oracle-bone inscriptions to the great seal script, and finally to the small seal script. Within this broad definition, seal script also comprises inscriptions found on tile ends, bricks, coins, measures, pottery, and, of course, seals up to the Qin dynasty. It is generally agreed among scholars that clerical script, or *lishu*, began to be used shortly before and during the Qin dynasty on prosaic documents but did not come into widespread use until the Han period. Thus, seal script encompasses the major script forms in the ancient and formative period of Chinese civilization and carries with it an aura of antiquity.

One of the most celebrated pieces of seal-script calligraphy from ancient China is the inscription on the Stone Drums from the state of Qin, generally datable to the fifth century B.C.[17] Since the discovery of the Stone Drums in the early Tang dynasty (618-906), they have inspired many eulogies and emulations. Both the Tang poet Han Yu (768-824) and the Song man-of-letters Su Shi (1037-1101) composed poems about them. For instance, Han Yu wrote:

> Time has not yet vanquished the beauty
>   of these letters—
> Looking like sharp daggers that pierce
>   live crocodiles,
> Like phoenix mates dancing, like angels
>   hovering down,
> Like trees of jade and coral with interlocking
>   branches,
> Like golden cord and iron chain tied together
>   tight,
> Like incense-tripods flung in the sea, like
>   dragons mounting heaven.[18]

The partially damaged stone drums are now in the Palace Museum, Beijing. Accessible to calligraphers and connoisseurs in the form of rubbings (for example, No. 1, Pl. 1), the writing has been called the Stone Drum Inscription (*shiguwen*). Its script is in a transitional form between the more robust and modulated great seal script and the more regulated small seal script and is characterized by strong, thick lines, stout proportions, and energy-laden execution.[19] A concrete embodiment of the Chinese ideal of antiquity, it was to inspire the calligraphy and seal engraving of such masters as Wang Shu (1668-1739), Wu Dacheng (1835-1902), Wu Changshuo (1844-1927; Nos. 31, 32, 33, 34, 52, 62) and Zhao Shuru (1874-1945; Nos. 37, 63). Wu Changshuo made many free-hand copies or interpretations of this inscription. His ostensible copies are often, in fact, re-creations derived from a combination of *shiguwen* and bronze inscriptions; the results are often monumental in configuration but moist and rich in brushwork (No. 62, Pl. 3).

Pl. 3, (No. 62). Wu Changshuo (1844-1927), **After the Ten Stone Drums Inscription**. Dated 1925. Hanging scroll.
Dr. and Mrs. Clyde Wu

In 221 B.C., Qin Shihuangdi had an imperial edict engraved and cast on weights and measures throughout his empire not only to unify standards but also to proclaim his political authority. The edict was written in a form that combined the smooth and elegant small seal script with the more angular clerical script. The overall configuration of the inscription, full of vitality both in the composition of the whole piece and in the structure of individual characters, was to serve as a model for many later seal engravers.[20]

Apart from its aesthetic appeal, seal script has been favored by later engravers because, for the thousand years preceding the third century B.C., seal script was utilized on monuments of power, ideology, and authority and thus became associated with the cultural history of ancient China. After the third century B.C., seal script was still utilized on monuments resulting in the persistence of antiquity and its use in seal engraving. Thus, seal script has become a symbol for the Chinese regard for the past as part of the present, something not to be left behind forever but to be used constantly to serve the present. During the period from the Han to the Tang dynasty, seal script was used in the title-head of stelae, *bei'e*. This led to a similar practice in calligraphy and painting. In later times there developed the custom of inscribing the title or frontispiece of a painting or piece of calligraphy with seal script, as in Wu Yi's (1472-1519) frontispiece to the handscroll *Enjoying the Pines* in the style of Shen Zhou in the Metropolitan Museum of Art (No. 55; Pl. 4) and Xu Lin's (1462-1538) frontispiece to Wen Zhengming's (1470-1559) handscroll *Autumn Mountain* in the Art Institute of Chicago (No. 54, Pl. 5). In both seals and the titles or frontispieces to other works of art, then, seal script functions as a special genre with its own conventions and aesthetic qualities. Moreover, it is also evident that seal engravers and calligraphers writing in seal script have long been practicing an art-historical art in which style functions as idea.[21]

Seal Script since the Han Dynasty and the Epigraphical Movement

By the time seal engraving came to be regarded as a special form of calligraphy in the theoretical writings of the literati around the fourteenth century, seal script had gone through a long history of development. Seal engravers and seal-script calligraphers, like many of their predecessors, were confronted with a perennial challenge: how to be creative while remaining true and responsible to the past.

One significant cultural characteristics of seal engraving is its archaism (*fugu*), that is, the perpetuation of ancient script types that are no longer used for most quotidian functions. Wen Fong has stated that "in *fugu* the Chinese saw history not as a long fall from grace, but as an enduring crusade to restore life and truth to art. Ancient models were seen in a non-historical continuum, in which the later man, should he succeed in achieving an inner response (*shenhui*, or 'spiritual correspondence') to his model, suddenly emerged as an equal rather than a follower."[22]

In the eighteenth century, seal script enjoyed an unprecedented popularity among scholars in a renascence of seal-script calligraphy and a flourishing of seal engraving. The main reason was the phenomenon of evidential research, or *kaozheng* studies, in which scholars turned to philology and epigraphy in search of the truth about ancient Chinese thought. As the eminent scholar Qian Daxin (1728-1804) put it: "For the most part, writings on bamboo and silk deteriorated rapidly over time. In the process of re-copying [these writings]

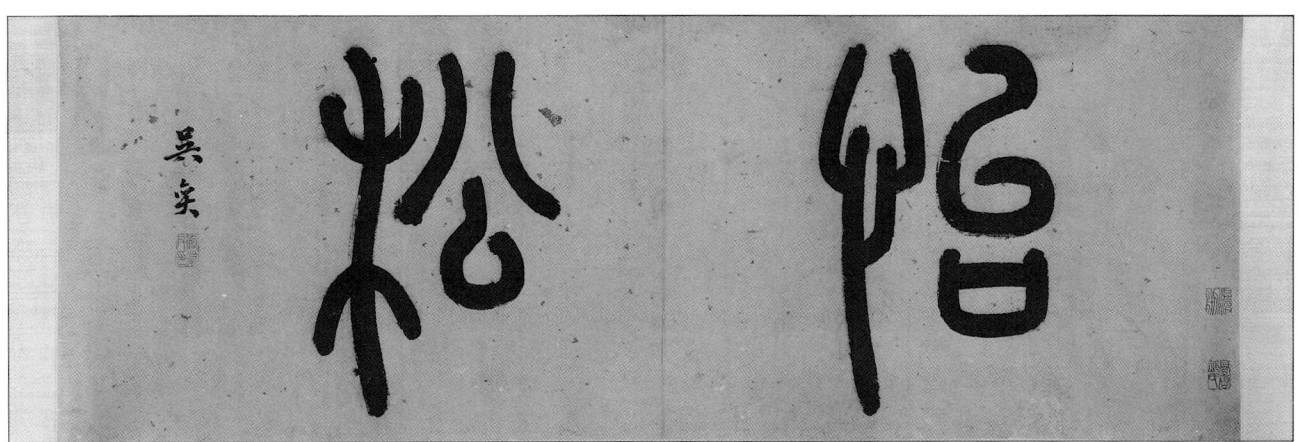

Pl. 4, (No. 55). Wu Yi (1472-1519), **Enjoying the Pines**. Calligraphy frontispiece to *Landscape in the style of Shen Zhou*. Section of a handscroll. The Metropolitan Museum of Art, New York; Bequest of John M. Crawford, Jr., 1988

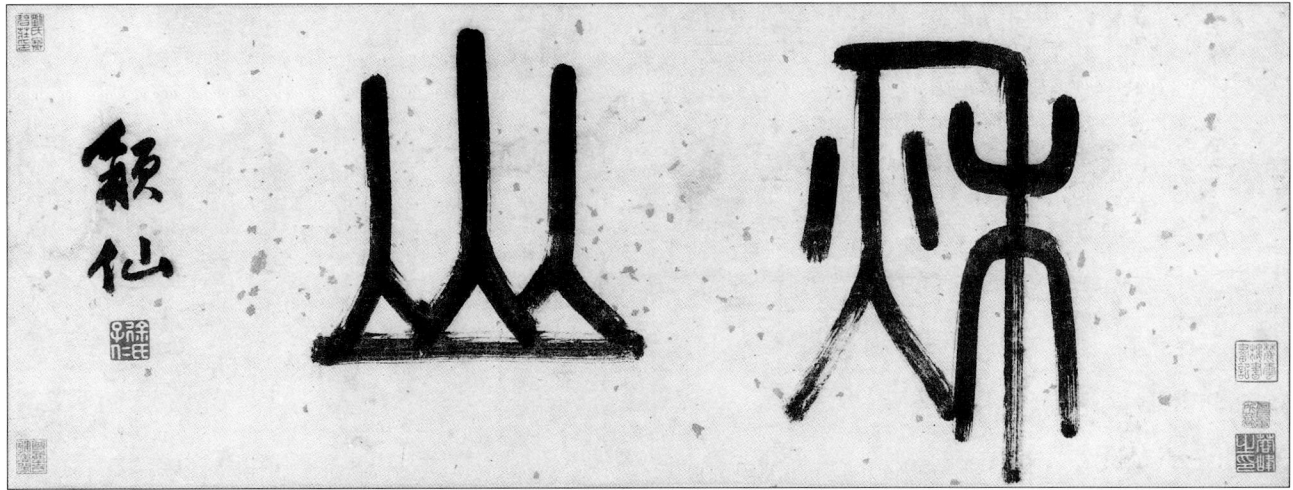

Pl. 5, (No. 54). Xu Lin (1462-1538), **Frontispiece to "Autumn Mountain" by Wen Zhengming**. Section of a handscroll. The Art Institute of Chicago, Kate S. Buckingham Fund, 1948.103

by hand over and over again, their original appearance was lost. Only bronze and stone inscriptions survive from hundreds and thousands of years ago. In them, we see the real appearance of the ancients. Both the writings [of this type] and the affairs [described in them] are reliable and verifiable. Therefore they are prized."[23] Books on seals (such as No. 50, Pl. 7), clay sealings (such as No. 51, Pls. 8, 9), and coins (such as No. 3, Pl. 6) were published under the influence of the *kaozheng* studies and exerted a strong influence on the development of seal engraving.[24]

This reverential attitude toward inscriptions on bronze and stone and the extensive studies of etymology and epigraphy carried out by renowned scholars in the seventeenth and eighteenth centuries stimulated a whole new school of calligraphic art—the Stele school, or *beixue pai*—and turned a new chapter in the history of Chinese calligraphy. The goal of the Stele school, sometimes called the Bronze-and-Stone Studies school, or *jinshixue pai*, was to study inscriptions found on bronze vessels and stelae dating from the Qin to the Tang dynasties (mainly through rubbings made from these monuments) in order to understand the original or authentic styles of early masters. Advocates of the Stele school tried to elevate the robust monumentality of the bronze and stele inscriptions over the refinement of calligraphy executed on paper or silk. To them, the calligraphic style derived from writings on paper or silk by masters in the Wang Xizhi tradition, called *tiexue*, was tied to the Examination-hall Style, or *guangeti*, the over-precise, over-refined, and often monotonous style of calligraphy favored by many Ming and Qing emperors and

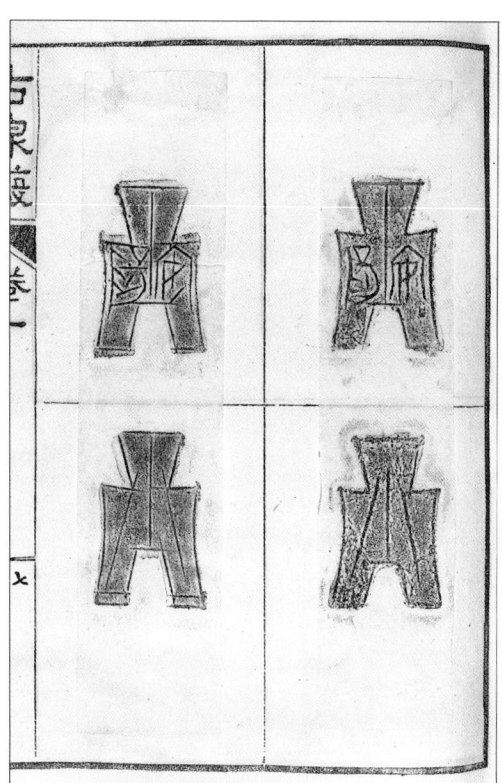

Pl. 6, (No. 3). Yang Shoujing (1839-1914), compiler, **Guquansou**. Leaf from a woodblock printed book. Gest Oriental Library and East Asian Collections, Princeton University, New Jersey

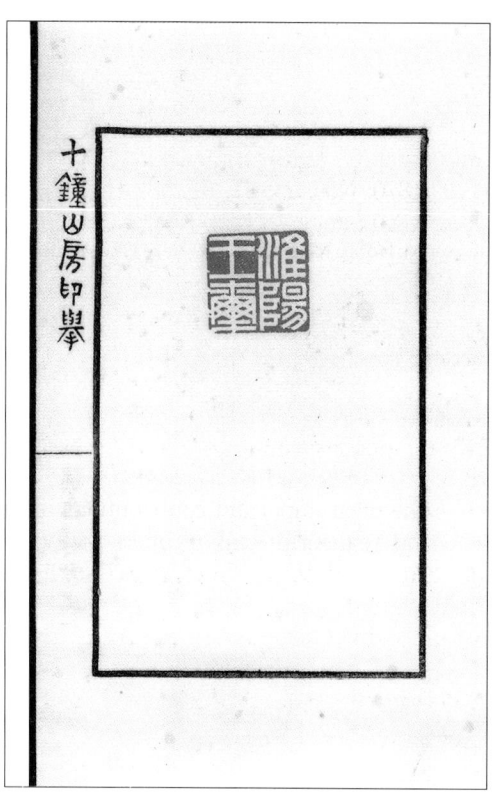

Pl. 7, (No. 50). Chen Jieqi (1813-1884), compiler, **Shizhong shanfang yinju**. Qing dynasty, first published 1872. Leaf from a woodblock printed book of seal impressions. Gest Oriental Library and East Asian Collections, Princeton University, New Jersey

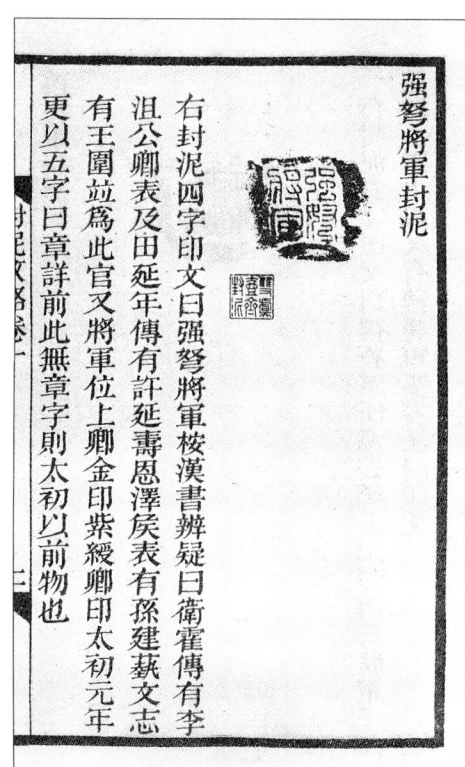

Pl. 8, (No. 51). Wu Shifen and Chen Jieqi, compilers, **Fengni Kaolue**. Qing dynasty, dated 1904. Verso leaf from a woodblock printed book of seal impressions. Gest Oriental Library and East Asian Collections, Princeton University, New Jersey

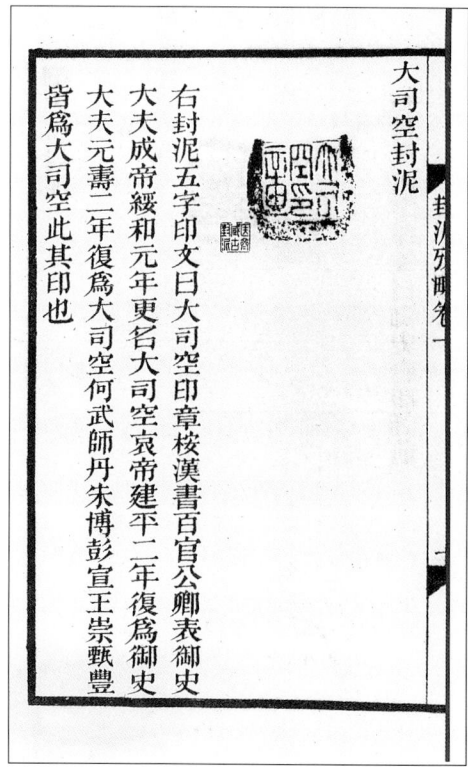

Pl. 9, (No. 51). Wu Shifen and Chen Jieqi, compilers, **Fengni Kaolue**. Qing dynasty, dated 1904. Recto leaf from a woodblock printed book of seal impressions. Gest Oriental Library and East Asian Collections, Princeton University, New Jersey

frequently employed to write imperial proclamations. One of the most important results was the revival and reinvigoration of seal-script calligraphy and seal engraving, and incidentally of painting.[25] The works of Sun Xingyan (1753-1818), Qian Dian (1741-1806), Wu Xizai (1799-1870; Nos. 24, 47, 57, 58), He Shaoji (1799-1873; No. 59), Xu Sangeng (1826-1890; Nos. 25, 61), Zhao Zhiqian (1829-1884; Nos. 27, 60), Wu Changshuo (1844-1927; Nos. 31, 32, 33, 34, 52, 62), Huang Binhong (1864-1955; No. 66), Qi Baishi (1863-1957; No. 64, 65), and Qiao Dazhuang (1892-1948; Nos. 40A, B), to name but a few, were examples of the importance of the contribution to the development of the art of seal engraving made by the study of bronze-and-stone inscriptions in general and seal script in particular.

One of the most important contributions of the seal engravers and seal-script calligraphers of the Bronze-and-Stone Studies school was their search for authenticity in their study, interpretation, and re-creation of ancient seal script, particularly when the script form itself was continuing to evolve and manifested a multitude of configurations—in other words, their search for honesty of form in seal script. Shen C. Y. Fu has observed that although the late Qing artists worked primarily from rubbings of inscriptions, "they sought to recapture this honesty in brush-written forms, not merely by imitation, visual allusion, or personal embellishment, but by an absorption so complete that their subsequent interpretations were valid transformations of the original. The composition, the spacing, the mode and energy of the brushwork became interpretations in the mind of the calligrapher in search of the ideal balance and proportion within the limitations of the chosen script and model. Each character therefore represented a defined range of aesthetic choices; yet the calligrapher was composing a fresh work, using the harmonies, rhythms, and cadences of the earlier mode. This was essentially the method and approach which emerged as the matrix of later Chinese calligraphy and painting."[26]

In writing seal script the brush is generally "held rigidly upright, the tip of the brush carefully maintained within the center of the stroke, and each stroke is written evenly and with powerful deliberation, as if inscribing lines in sand with a sharp stick (*ruzhui huasha*)."[27] The hidden or restrained tip of the brush "epitomizes an enduring cultural and artistic ideal: virtue, or strength—the sharp tip of the brush—is to be held within, guiding and shaping action."[28]

A seal engraver must first of all be a fine calligrapher. For without a mastery of calligraphy, particularly of the 9,353 characters (among which, more than four hundred are not easily constructed through the combination of radicals) in small seal script, as catalogued in the Han dictionary *Shuowen jiezi* by Xu Shen, a seal engraver is bound to exhibit ignorance and will be looked down upon by the learned in his audience. Wu Xizai's hand-annotated copy of *Shuowen jiezi* (Pl. 13, No. 49) exemplifies the attention paid to the Han dynasty

Pl. 10, (No. 2). **Coin**, inscribed *Qiubei* (Coin from the city of Qiu). Warring States Period (475-221 B.C.). Bronze. Yale University Art Gallery, New Haven; Gift of Professor and Mrs. Hans H. Frankel

work by serious seal engravers. Furthermore, since the late Qing period, seal engravers have been encouraged to incorporate many newly discovered ancient script types into the seal legends, i.e. the individual characters on the seal face, including the oracle bone and bronze-vessel scripts and scripts used for inscriptions on coins (No. 2, Pl. 10; No. 3, Pl. 6), tile ends (No. 4, Pl. 11), and bricks (Pl. 12, Fig. 2). Certainly, it was impossible to be a creative seal engraver without a deep knowledge of all kinds of ancient Chinese scripts.

Judging Seal Scripts and Carved Seals

One can judge the quality of a piece of seal-script calligraphy and an impression of a seal by similar criteria. A seal impression is, after all, a replica of a piece of calligraphy written and engraved on a flat surface but in reverse. One considers not only the quality of individual strokes, the spacing, and the composition as a whole, but also the relation of the characters to each other. Finally, one considers the way the seal script is interpreted. The interpretation of the script involves a study of the script form itself as well as a study of how master calligraphers and seal engravers of the past, each in his own turn, interpreted it. The appreciation and evaluation of seal engraving and seal-script calligraphy, like those of Chinese calligraphy in general, thus presupposes familiarity with the history of seal-script calligraphy since its early beginnings.

Beyond the cosmological and aesthetic ideals to be discussed below, certain specific principles of composition in seal engraving may be briefly presented.

A. Compositional Types

The seal engraver as artist is challenged by an art form that is concerned with the creation of a whole world on a very small surface under the constraints of the conventions of written Chinese characters. Besides having a well-rounded knowledge of philology and becoming accomplished as a calligrapher, the artist must be able to arrange the chosen characters within the restricted space of the seal face, to write them out in reverse, and to engrave them onto the surface of the seal. The requirements are very similar to those for a calligraphic scroll where *hangqi*, or "spirit of the lines," and *zhangfa*, or "compositional arrangement," must be carefully yet intuitively constructed. In composing the legend, the seal engraver must pay attention to not only the relationship of characters to the total surface but also the relationship between the characters as well as the internal composition of each character. With regard to the relationship between the characters, for instance, the viewer can determine whether it is unified or contrasted, whether close together or far apart, and how the vertical relationships interact with the horizontal ones.[29]

Several types of composition can be distinguished:

1. Balanced (Nos. 7, 21)
2. Spare/dense (No. 33; No. 52D, Pl. 14)
3. All-white (Nos. 52E, F, Pl. 14)
4. Silver (white) thread/gold (red) thread
5. Boundary (No. 52C, Pl. 14)
6. Sparse Composition (Nos. 52N, R, Pl. 14)
7. Border-touching (Nos. 52M, N, T, Pl. 14)
8. Borderless (No. 52G, Pl. 14)
9. Red-and-white, or "mandarin duck" (No. 22)

B. Construction of Characters

In the art of seal engraving, the construction of characters is fundamental to the composition. Because the characters must adhere to convention in order to convey their semantic meaning while maintaining the formal and rhythmic qualities appropriate to seal engraving, the principles of construction of characters in seal engraving are more or less the same as those in calligraphy. For example, in *Shupu*, the treatise on calligraphy, dated 697, by the great Tang calligrapher Sun Guoting,

Pl. 11, (No. 4). **Molded Pottery Tile Terminal**. Han dynasty (3rd c. B.C.). Field Museum of Natural History, Chicago; no. 118944A (neg. no. A97697)

it is suggested that in composing a piece of calligraphy and in constructing a character "the beginner should first aim at conformity and moderation, after which he goes upon perilous ways, and later comes to moderation and conformity once more."[30] As in written calligraphy, in order appreciate the composition of a seal legend the viewer can study the characters' shapes as normal or distorted, stubby or elongated, strongly slanted or having a more horizontal or vertical configuration (Nos. 52D, M, R, Pl. 14).

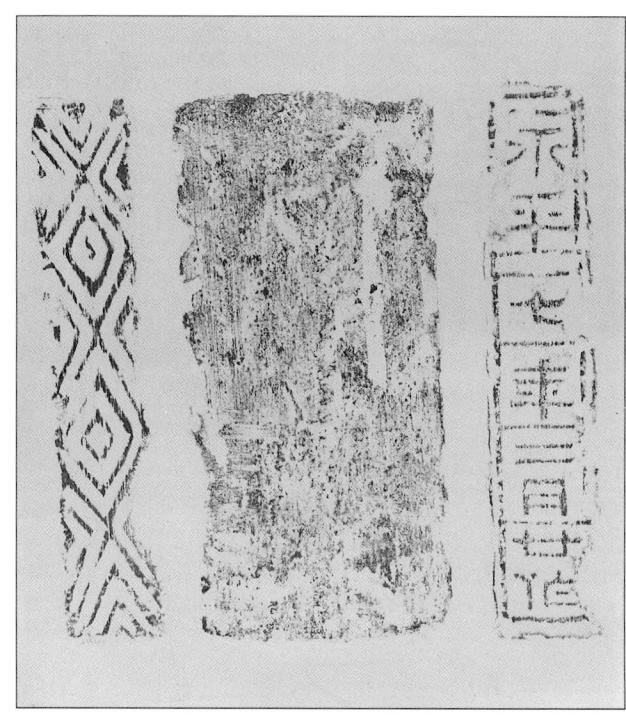

Pl. 12 (Fig. 2). **Rubbing of a Brick with Inscription**. Field Museum of Natural History, Chicago, no. 233600 (neg. no. A111830). The inscription reads: "[This brick has been] manufactured on the twentieth day of the second month, in the seventh year of the Yongping reign [A.D. 64]."

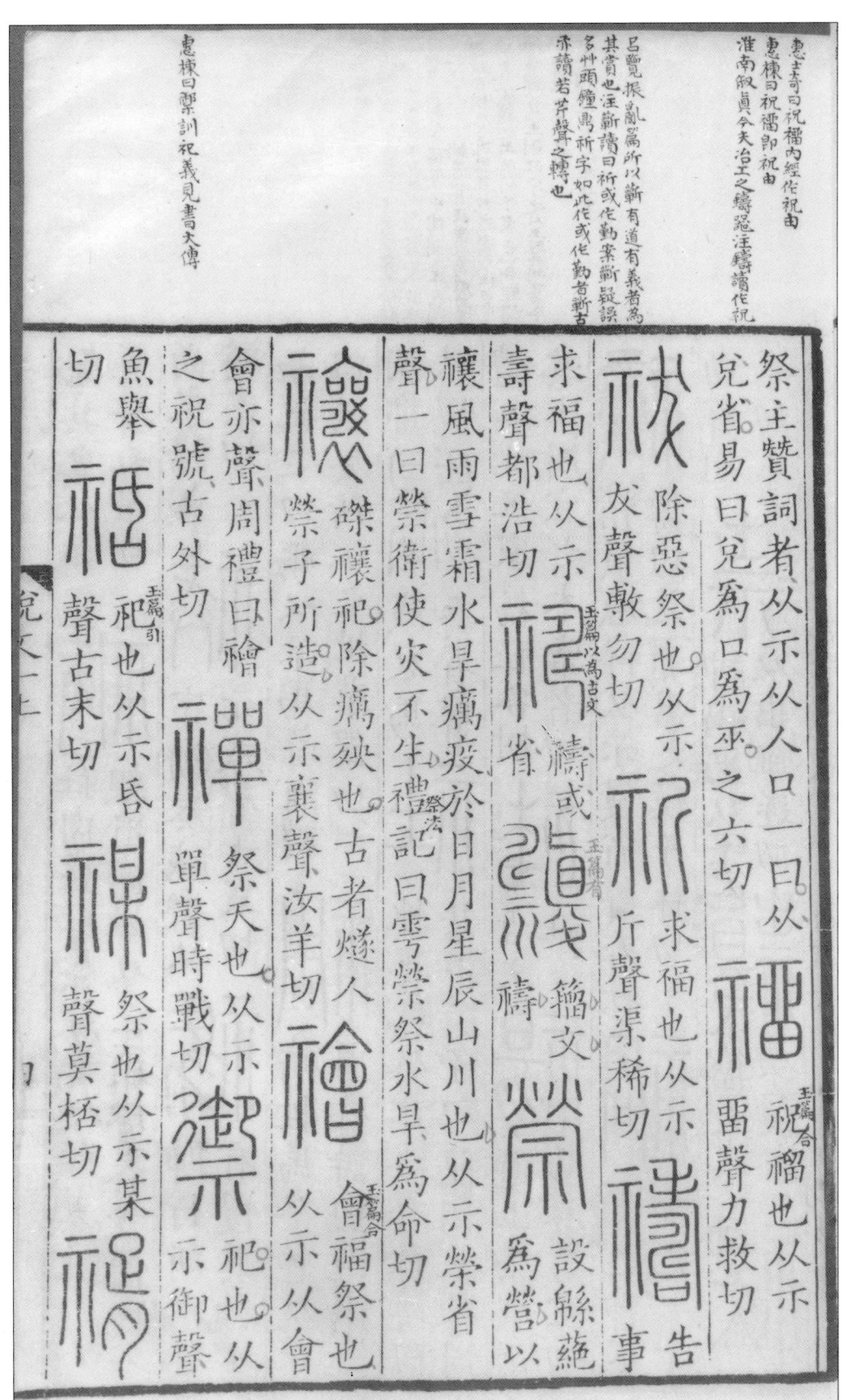

Pl. 13, (No. 49). **"Shuowen jiezi" by Xu Shen with hand-written annotations by Wu Xizai**. Ming dynasty, 17th c. Leaf from a woodblock printed book with hand-written notes in ink. Wang Fang-yu and Sum Wai Wang

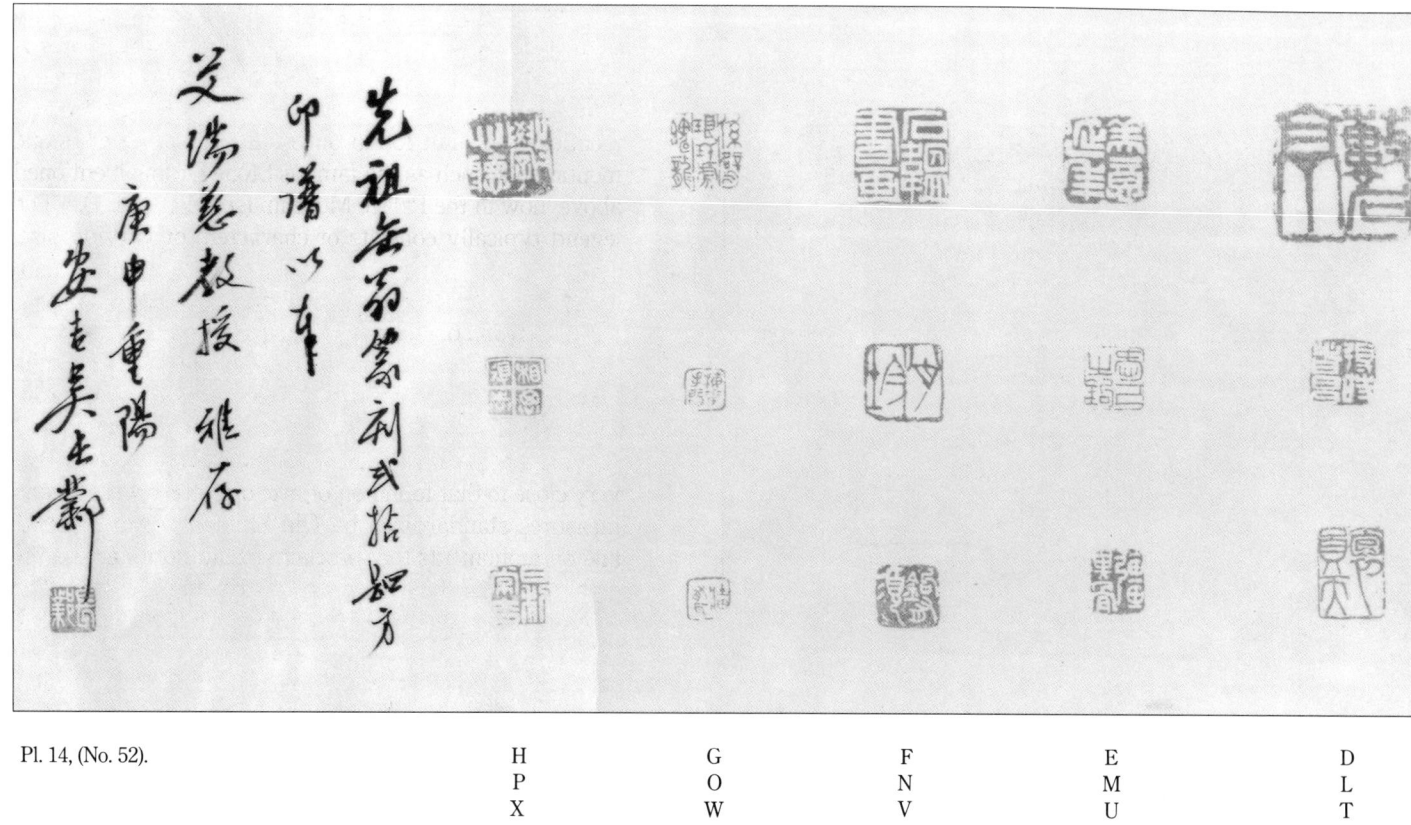

Pl. 14, (No. 52).

Wu Changshuo (1844-1927), **Handscroll of seal impressions**. Ink on paper. Chien Lu Collection

Before presenting a brief history of the art of seal engraving in China, it is important to point out a few obvious differences between seal engraving and calligraphy. Wang Fang-yu has observed that the scripts used on seals are often pre-Han scripts; they are engraved on a small surface in the shape of a square, rectangle, ellipsis, circle, or an odd shape; and the size is generally one-quarter to five inches in width. Whereas calligraphy is generally executed large and in the multiple formats of handscroll, hanging scroll or album, and customarily written on paper or silk and occasionally onto stone, seals can be engraved on all kinds of material (stone, ivory, wood, bamboo, bronze, and so forth).[31]

SEAL ENGRAVING AND ITS DEVELOPMENT

The Earliest Seals: Pre-Qin and Qin Periods

The earliest seals have been traced back to the Shang dynasty. Three bronze seals, now in the National Palace Museum, have been ascribed to a Shang site in Anyang.[32] Although the legends on two of them are difficult to decipher, the third has a design bounded by a cross-shaped cartouche such as is found in inscriptions on Shang bronze vessels. The design consists of a bird on top and a trap at the bottom; the combination has been deciphered as the character *qin*—most likely, the owner's name or clan emblem. Unfortunately, these seals have not been found through scientific excavations, and their authenticity remains in doubt. The practice of engraving inscriptions on oracle bones and casting inscriptions on ritual bronze vessels during the

Pl. 15, (from left to right) A: (No. 6). **Lacquer Seal**. Warring States Period (475-221 B.C.). B: (No. 5). **Silver Seal**. Warring States Period (475-221 B.C.). Dr. Paul Singer

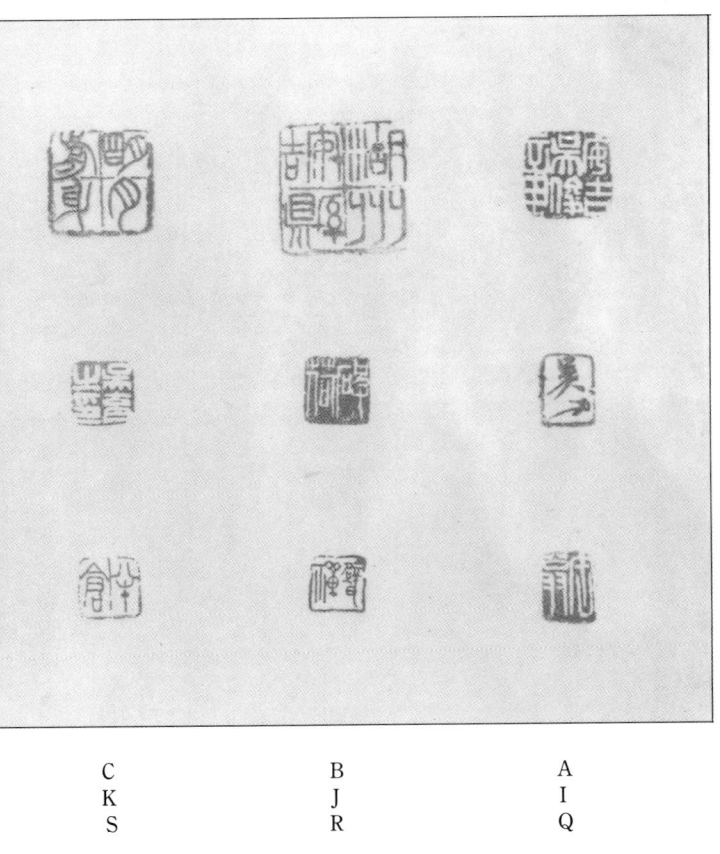

```
C        B        A
K        J        I
S        R        Q
```

Shang period laid the foundation for the beginning of the art of seal engraving in China. An example of another early technique similar to seal engraving is the engraved inscription on a stone musical instrument that was found in the tomb of Fuhao at Anyang.[33] Thus seal engraving probably had its precursor in writing from the earliest historical period of China.

Although the earliest extant seals can only be reliably dated from the Warring States period (480-221 B.C.), there are literary references which indicate that seal engraving in its embryonic form developed in the Spring and Autumn period (722-481 B.C.). In the *Zuozhuan*, a commentary on Confucius's *Spring and Autumn Annals* traditionally ascribed to Zuo Qiuming, a reference is made to the use of seal impressions on official documents in 544 B.C.; in the *Lüshi chunqiu* ascribed to Lü Buwei (d. 235 B.C.), a reference is made to the use of seals and sealing clays.[34] Tsien Tsuen-hsuin has observed that the lost-wax method of casting bronze suggested the "carving of writing in reverse [similar to seal engraving] to obtain a positive position on the object to be cast, as was later to be done in printing." For example, in the inscription on the ritual vessel, *Qingonggui*, which probably dates from the 7th century B.C., each character was cast from a separate unit, leaving the edges of the units to form a grid. Similarly, each of the characters of the inscription on the bell, *Qizizhong*, was cast from an individual mold.[35]

Apart from examples with pictorial legends, early seals were for the most part engraved on hard materials or cast of bronze with ideograms. During the Warring States period, the script used on seals is more or less identical with that found on bronze vessels or on stone monuments, such as the famous Stone Drums mentioned above, now in the Palace Museum (see No. 1, Pl. 1).[36] The legend typically consists of characters of varying size, and the composition of the whole legend, as well as the construction of individual characters, tends to be irregular (Nos. 5 and 6, Pl. 15). Often the legend is confined to a border. Both relief and intaglio scripts were used, sometimes in the same seal legend. The shape of the seal face can be square, rectangular, or round.

During the Qin dynasty, the script used on seals is very close to that found on bronze or pottery weights and measures standardized by Qin Shihuangdi in 221 B.C. and on monuments that proclaim his authority across the empire.[37] Often the legend was distributed in a grid. The characters are generally in intaglio and tend to be more regular in size than those on seals of the Warring States period, although from time to time the regularity gave way to compositional needs. Qin seals are mostly square, although rectangular seals were also used.

The Qin dynasty provided still another source of inspiration for later seal engravers: the inscriptions on pottery bricks and tile ends. Of particular interest to later seal engravers are the circular tile ends on which auspicious phrases were impressed; sometimes the names of palaces and government buildings were also impressed on these tile ends. A tile end (No. 4, Pl. 16) with an inscription reading *changle wei yang* (happy forever, without end), probably from the Qin dynasty, is now in

Pl. 16, (No. 4). **Ink Rubbing of Tile Terminal**. Qin or Han dynasty (3rd c. B.C.). Field Museum of Natural History, Chicago; no. 118944B (neg. no. A97698)

27

Pl. 17, (No. 13). **Three Clay Impressions of Pictorial Seals**.
Han dynasty (206 B.C.-A.D. 220) seals; modern impressions.
Private collection

the Field Museum of Natural History in Chicago.[38] It is the seeming naïveté and unpretentiousness of the seals of the pre-Qin and Qin periods, as discussed above, that were to inspire the literati seal engravers of later periods.

Seals and Seal Script of the Han Dynasty

Seals dating from the Han dynasty—discovered in great quantity—have been regarded as paradigms in the art of seal engraving (Nos. 7, 8, 9, 10, 11, 12, 13, 14, 50, and 51). As the Qing writer Wu Xiansheng put it, "In seal engraving, one must follow that of the Han dynasty, just as in poetry one must learn from the Tang dynasty, and in calligraphy one must learn from the Jin dynasty."[39] Made by anonymous calligraphers, Han seals display many of the qualities that were considered desirable by early writers on the art of seal engraving.

Han seals can be divided into two kinds according to their functions. Official seals were used by ministers and bureaucrats as emblems of authority and for authenticating documents (No. 12, Pl. 20). Private seals with the names of their owners were used by individuals in more personal documents (Nos. 7, 8, 9, and 14). Pictorial seals were mostly used as private seals (No. 10; No. 13, Pl. 17; and No. 11, Pl. 18).

The knob of a seal was usually in the shape of an animal (No. 11, Pl. 18; No. 14, Color pl. 1) or a simple loop (Nos. 7, 8, 9, 10, Pl. 19) allowing for the attachment of a cord. Some seals were engraved or cast with characters in reverse in intaglio on its face (*mian*). When stamped on paper or silk with red ink, these seal impressions show white characters (hence the term *baiwen*) against a red background (No. 14; No. 50, Pl. 7). The characters on other seals were engraved or cast, also in reverse, in relief. When stamped on paper or silk with red ink, these impressions show red characters (hence the term *zhuwen*) against a plain background.

During the Han dynasty, particularly before the extensive use of paper in the third century, documents were often written on bamboo and wooden tablets. These tablets were bound with string and "sealed" with a wad of clay. These sealing clays, called *fengni* or *nifeng*, bear the impressions of official seals and have been a great resource for the art of seal engraving as well as the study of geography and government (No. 12, Pl. 20; No. 51, Pls. 8, 9). Many of the seals by Zhao Zhiqian (No. 27) and Wu Changshuo (No. 52, Pl. 14; Nos. 32, 33, 34) were inspired by the blunt and archaic beauty of *fengni*.

A similar resource for the seal engraver are the impressed workshop marks on pottery found in Shanxi, Henan, and Hebei provinces.[40] It is significant that the phrase *ruyin yinni* (like seals stamping on clay) was one of the desiderata in the criticism of Chinese calligraphy first expounded by Chu Suiliang (596-658) of the Tang

Pl. 18, (No. 11). **Pictorial Seal**, two views. Han dynasty (206 B.C.-A.D. 220). Bronze. Dr. Paul Singer

Pl. 19, (from left to right) A: (No. 7). **Jade Seal**. Han dynasty (206 B.C.-A.D. 220). B: (No. 8). **Jade Seal**. Han dynasty (206 B.C.-A.D. 220). C: (No. 9). **Jade Seal**. Han dynasty (206 B.C.-A.D. 220). D: (No. 10). **Pictorial Seal**. Han dynasty (206 B.C.-A.D. 220). Jade. Dr. Paul Singer

dynasty and was inspired by the use of sealing clay. The phrase has long been used by critics to praise a master calligrapher's virtual penetration of paper or silk with the energy of a seal stamping its impression into the clay.

During the Han dynasty, in place of the small seal script codified in the Qin dynasty, two other script types were more commonly used on seals. One was called sinuous seal script, or *miaozhuan* (Nos. 7, 8); the other was called bird-and-insect script, or *niaochongshu*.

Strongly influenced by clerical script which was in wide use during the Han dynasty, characters in sinuous seal script can be square or rectangular in shape and can have a reduced or increased number of strokes in order to accommodate the composition of the seal legend. Sinuous seal script was also found in such famous stelae as the *Sisangongshan bei* (dated A.D. 117), the *Kaimumiao shiqueming* (dated A.D. 123), and the *Shaoshi shiqueming* (dated A.D. 123), as well as in bricks and tile ends.[41] In the *Sisangongshan bei*, for instance, the characters are basically in seal script modified by clerical script: the round brushwork of the seal script is modified by the angular brushwork of the clerical script. Seal script is also sometimes modified by running script. As we shall see, the inscriptions on these stelae have had a substantial influence on such seal engravers as Qi Baishi (Nos. 35, 36, 53, 65, and 64).

The bird-and-insect script, which was mentioned by Xu Shen in his *Shuowen jiezi*, was developed earlier—during the Eastern Zhou dynasty—and is found inlaid on such bronzes as the recently excavated swords from the state of Yue.[42] In the Han dynasty, it was used on such vessels as a *hu* dated to the second half of the second century B.C., from the tomb of Liu Sheng at Mancheng, Hebei Province.[43] Both sinuous seal script and bird-and-insect script are very ornate and stylized, indicating an increasing self-consciousness in the designing of seals as aesthetic objects.[44]

In general, the character strokes on official Han seals are angular, with a slight touch of roundness. This was probably the result of having to accommodate the essentially round strokes of seal script within the format of the seal, which in most cases was either square or rectangular. Another reason was the intrusion of the now more popular clerical script, in which predominantly angular and flaring strokes create characters whose configuration tend to be squat or horizontally rectangular. The transformation of seal script from a script with rounded brushwork of more or less even thickness into the sinuous seal script during the Han dynasty is an indication of the self-renewal of the early Chinese writing system and an example of "the inconsistency of character structure in Chinese writing."[45]

Equilibrium and harmony were achieved in such typical Han seals as the three examples from the collection of Dr. Paul Singer (Nos. 7, 8, and 9). In general, both the sinuous seal script and bird-and-insect script found on seals and other kinds of impressed inscriptions from the Han dynasty (No. 12, Pl. 20; Fig. 2, Pl. 12; No. 51, Pls. 8, 9) have been treasured by literati seal engravers for their seeming naïveté and ingenious spacing of the characters.

Pl. 20, (No. 12). **Clay Seal Impression**. Han dynasty (206 B.C.-A.D. 220). Field Museum of Natural History, Chicago; no. 117030 (neg. no. A97972)

Seal Engraving and Seal-Script Calligraphy from the Six Dynasties to the Ming Dynasty

After the Han dynasty, the art of seal engraving and seal-script calligraphy suffered a period of general decline. Seals tended to be crudely cast (No. 15, Pl. 21; No. 17, Pl. 22; No. 18, Pl. 23) and seal script at times was too ornate (No. 19). Even the legends and designs on seals used by such a master of calligraphy as Mi Fu seemed hesitant and undistinguished.[46] As for seal-script calligraphy, Li Yangbin (active 759-780?) seemed to be one of the few who were able to revive the vigor of the Qin-dynasty style. His curved strokes, which predominate over angular ones, tend to be balanced, clear, precise, and symmetrical.

Although seals had been used by calligraphers since the Tang dynasty and by painters since the Northern Song dynasty, it was during the Yuan dynasty (1280-1368) that treatises on seal engraving as an art form appeared. The most important treatise was *Sanshiwuju* by Wu Yan, also known as Wu Qiuyan (1272-1311).[47] Wu's seal engraving, like his seal-script calligraphy, was mostly inspired by Han-dynasty models.[48]

Zhao Mengfu (1254-1322), Wu Qiuyan's older contemporary, was an accomplished calligrapher and painter whose large seal script adorns the frontispieces of several examples of his calligraphy in regular script. Although he seemed to have had his seals engraved by others, he was known for his espousal of a particularly slender and elegant seal script that is essentially round in its configuration (hence the term *yuanzhuwen*, or round-relief script) in the seals he used on his own calligraphy and painting, such as his handscroll *Twin Pines on a Flat Vista* at The Metropolitan Museum of Art (Pl. 24, Fig. 3).[49] As opposed to the extremely complicated script called *jiudiewen*, or nine-bended script, commonly used on official seals during the Song dynasty,[50] *yuanzhuwen*, with its clarity and elegance, could be seen as an embodiment of Zhao Mengfu's archaism favoring simplicity and naturalism.

Wang Mian (d. 1359), the famous Yuan dynasty painter of ink plum blossoms, was traditionally credited for beginning the use of soft soapstone to engrave seals, although archaeological evidence suggests that soapstone was used for seals as early as the Han dynasty.[51] Some of his seals recapture the hastily but spontaneously engraved bronze seals used by Han-dynasty generals.[52] Thereafter, other seal engravers would emulate not only the rugged forcefulness of Han seals but also the random damage and deterioration through age to the legends of these haste seals (*jijiuzhang*) in order to suggest antiquity and intentional awkwardness (*guzhuo*), qualities admired by literati starting in the Yuan dynasty.

It was during the later part of the Ming dynasty (1368-1644) that seal engraving attained a high status

Pl. 21, (No. 15). **Official Seal with Figure of Reclining Camel as Knob**. Wei Dynasty (Three Kingdoms Period [221-65]). Bronze. Field Museum of Natural History, Chicago; no. 117044 (neg. no. A111831)

Pl. 22, (No. 17). **Official Seal**. Song dynasty, dated 1055. Bronze. Field Museum of Natural History, Chicago; no. 117059 (neg. no. A111832)

Pl. 23, (No. 18). **Official Seal**. Yuan dynasty, dated 1308. Bronze. Field Museum of Natural History, Chicago; no. 117065 (neg. no. A111833)

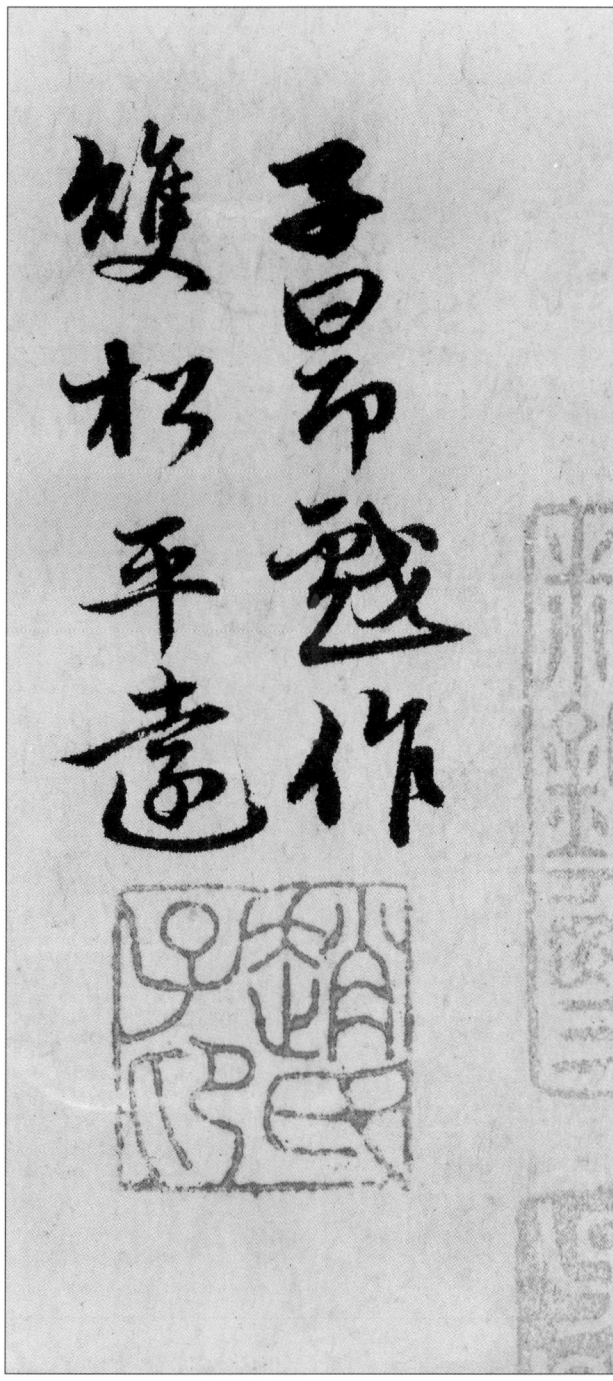

Pl. 24 (Fig. 3). Zhao Mengfu (1254-1322), **Twin Pines and Flat Vista**. Detail of a handscroll, ink on paper. The Metropolitan Museum of Art, New York; Gift of the Dillon Fund, 1973

among the literati. James C. Y. Watt has observed that "for the first time, it was possible to distinguish oneself by the practice of this art form alone, and the work of those literati who specialized in it was much in demand; no longer was it artistically or socially acceptable to use seals that showed no qualities of learning and taste."[53]

Two of the most important seal engravers of the period were Wen Peng and He Zhen. Each is regarded as the founder of a distinct school of seal engraving.

Wen Peng (1498-1573) was the oldest son of Wen Zhengming (1470-1599), one of the greatest calligrapher-painters of the Ming dynasty and one of the leaders of the Wu school of painting that dominated sixteenth-century China. The son concentrated his energy on seal engraving rather than on painting. Because of his fame, there have been a large number of forged seals ascribed to him. The seals that follow his calligraphy in The Metropolitan Museum of Art (No. 56, Pl. 25), however, are good examples of his style. Wen Peng also engraved many of the seals used by his father Wen Zhengming and his younger brother Wen Jia (1501-1583).[54]

He Zhen (ca. 1530-ca. 1604) was the founder of the Hui, or Wan (Anhui), school of seal engraving. His seal engraving was equated with that of the ancients by the seventeenth-century scholar Xu Shipu (1608-1685), as quoted by Zhou Lianggong (1612-1672), a great art patron and a connoisseur of seal engraving. According to Xu, He Zhen's seal engraving was as important as the calligraphy and painting of Dong Qichang (1555-1636), the astronomy of Xu Guangqi (1562-1633) and Matteo Ricci (1552-1610), the poetry and drama of Tang Xianzu (1550-1617), the pharmacology of Li Shizhen (1518-1633), and the philology of Zhao Huanguang (1559-1625), among others.[55] His art was deeply grounded in his study of philology and the archaic simplicity of Han-dynasty seals.

Seal-script calligraphy also began to regain importance beginning in the mid-Ming dynasty. Many good examples, such as those by Xu Lin (1462-1538; No. 54, Pl. 5) and Wu Yi (1472-1519; No. 55, Pl. 4), exist as frontispieces to other paintings or pieces of calligraphy.

Masters of Seal Engraving and Seal-Script Calligraphy of the Qing Dynasty

During the Qing dynasty, as mentioned above, the development of seal engraving gained momentum due to the phenomenon called Evidential Research, or *kaozheng* studies in philology and epigraphy. For instance, Ding Jing (1695-1765), founder of the Zhe (Zhejiang) school of seal engraving, was an avid collector of rubbings of ancient inscriptions. He advised Wang Qishu (1728-1800) in the compilation of the seal book *Feihongtang yinpu* (No. 44, Pl. 60). Clearly, the seal engravings by Chen Lian (1730-1778; No. 45, Pl. 57) were based on a conscious effort to emulate ancient seals and stone inscriptions, including the effects of weathering and damage.

The Eight Masters of Xiling refers to Ding Jing and his followers. Noteworthy among his followers was Huang Yi (1744-1802), a dedicated epigrapher who traveled extensively in search of extant examples of ancient inscriptions. Huang tried to incorporate the method of clerical script as found in Han-dynasty seals into his own work (No. 21).[56] Other members of this group include Chen Hongshou (1768-1822; No. 22, Pl. 26),[57]

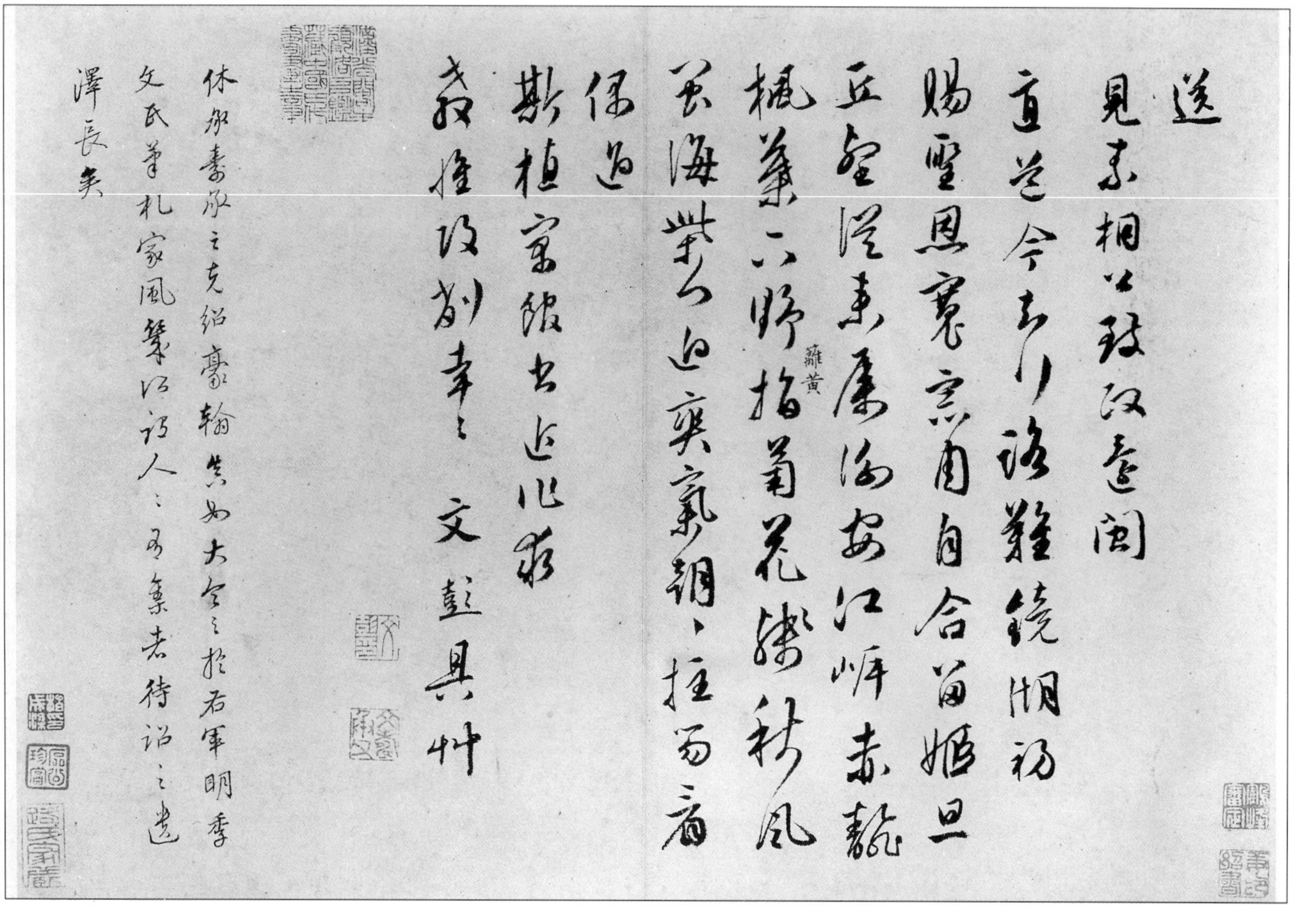

Pl. 25, (No. 56). Wen Peng (1498-1573), **Draft Poem for Seeing Off Lin Jun**. Ming dynasty, datable to 1523. Large album leaf. The Metropolitan Museum of Art, New York; Bequest of John M. Crawford, Jr., 1988

Zhao Zhichen (1781-1852; No. 23, Pl. 42),[58] Jiang Ren, Xi Gang, Chen Yuzhong, and Qian Song (1818-1860; No. 26, Color pl. 5).[59]

Whereas Ding Jing founded the Zhe school, Deng Shiru (1743-1805) founded the Deng school. He was also considered a member of the Wan school founded by He Zhen because he came from Anhui. Deng Shiru was one of the most important figures of the Bronze-and-Stone Studies school of calligraphy in the eighteenth century. Strongly influenced by the round and smooth thin relief lines preferred by Zhao Mengfu, Deng Shiru's late seal engraving is characterized by a tight structure. In the best of his seal compositions, he was able to achieve an equilibrium of void and solid and of sparsity and density, for which his seal-script calligraphy is also well known. His seal engravings strongly influenced Wu Xizai (1799-1870), Xu Sangeng (1806-1890), and Zhao Zhiqian (1829-1884).

Wu Xizai (No. 24, Pl. 29; No. 47, Color pls. 6A-C; No. 48, Pl. 27; No. 57, Pl. 28; No. 58, Color pl. 7) was a pupil of the calligrapher Bao Shichen (1775-1855), who in turn studied with Deng Shiru. According to Wu himself, he began to study Han seals at the age of fifteen; after fifteen years, he discovered the seal engraving of Deng

Pl. 26, (No. 22). Chen Hongshou (1768-1822), **Seal**. Qing dynasty. Shoushan stone. Wang Fang-yu and Sum Wai Wang

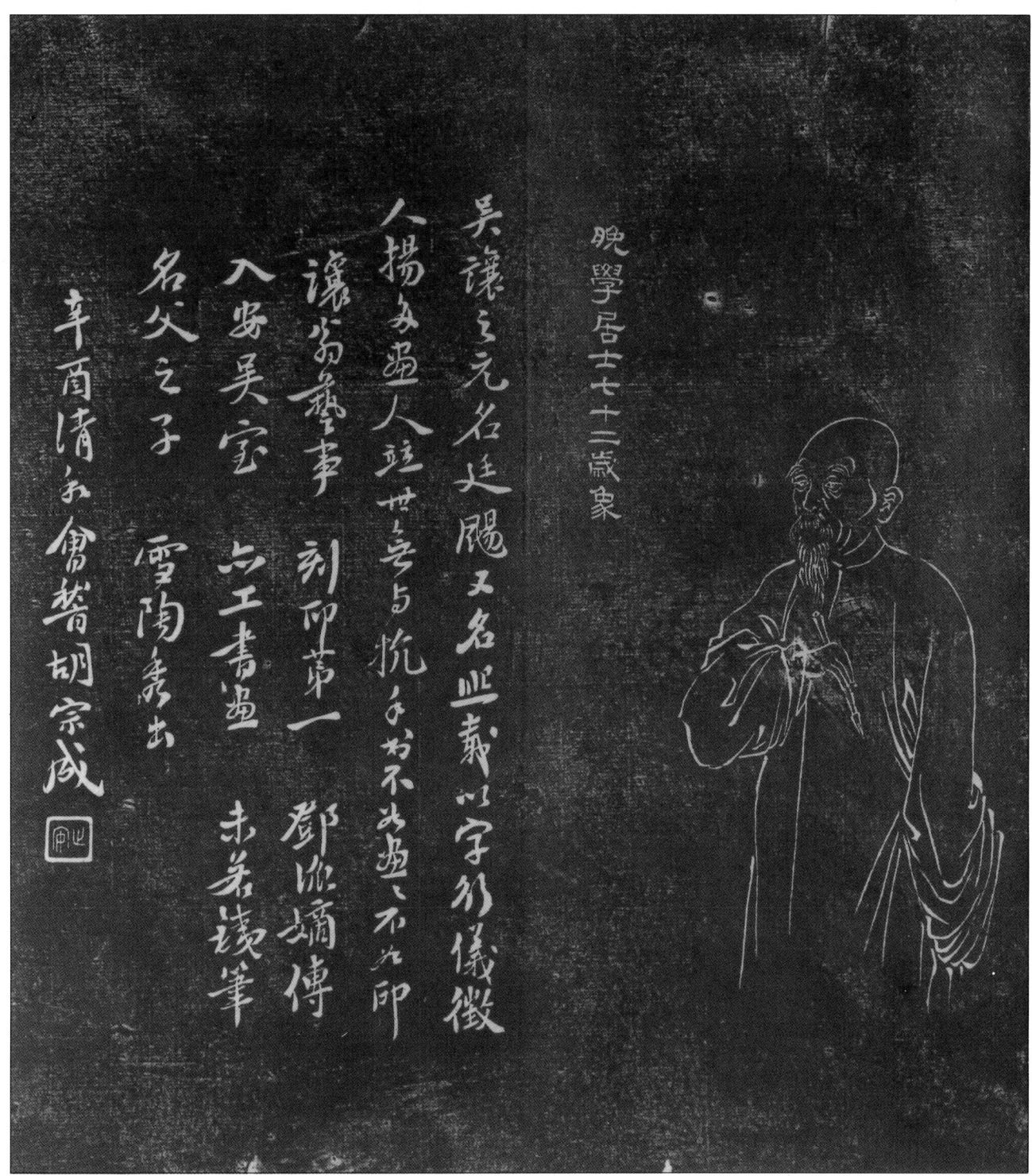

Pl. 27, (No. 48). Anonymous, **Portrait of Wu Xizai (Rangzhi)**. Qing dynasty, 19th c. Section of a handscroll, *Portraits of Seal Artists*, mounted as an album. Wang Fang-yu and Sum Wai Wang

Shiru and devoted himself to learning from Deng.[60] In addition to his diligent study of philology, as seen in his hand-annotated copy of *Shuowen jiezi*, by the Han scholar Xu Shen (No. 49, Pl. 13), Wu Xizai was also an accomplished calligrapher. His mastery of seal script can be seen in the set of four hanging scrolls transcribing the *Shijing*, or *Book of Songs* (No. 57, Pl. 28). In addition, his painting, with its strong planar emphasis, was another manifestation of the influence of the Bronze-and-Stone Studies school (No. 58, Color pl. 7). His seals in white characters (*baiwen*) tended to follow the monumental style of Han-dynasty sinuous seal script. His red-character-

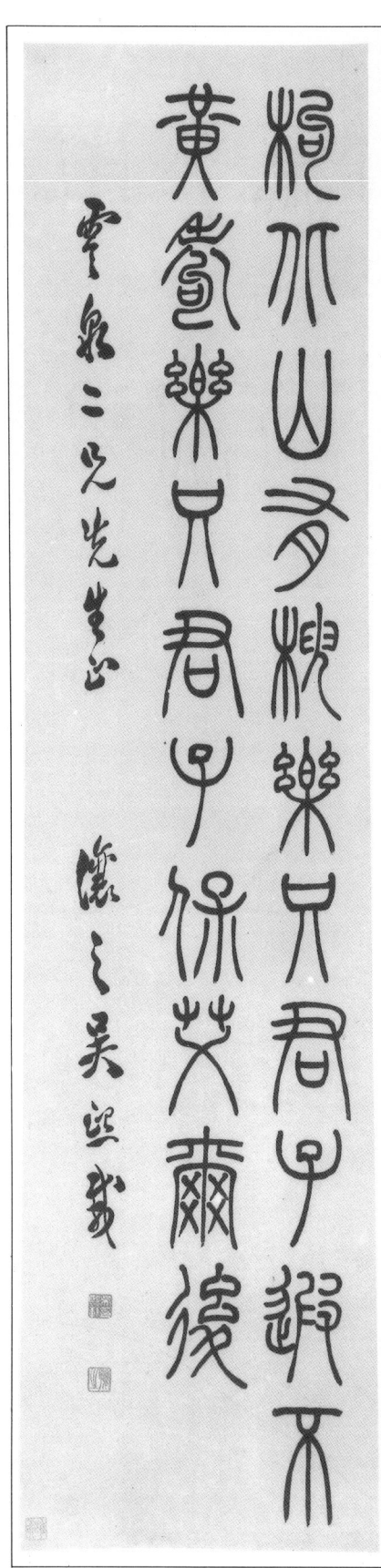

Pl. 28, (No. 57). Wu Xizai (1799-1870), **Transcription of "The Book of Songs."** Set of four hanging scrolls. F. Randall and Judith G. Smith

Pl. 29, (No. 24). Wu Xizai (1799-1870), **Seal**. Qing dynasty. Shoushan stone. Yi Lei Wang

impression (*zhuwen*) seals, however, tended to emphasize the flavor of the pliant brush. In his knife techniques, he combined thin and thick strokes to achieve a more varied effect (No. 24, Pl. 29).

He Shaoji (1799-1873) was one of the major calligraphers of the late Qing dynasty. Like many of his contemporaries, he made a conscientious study of stele inscriptions from various periods. In his late years, he tried to inject the style of seal script with clerical script, combining both in his running-cursive (*xingcao*) script calligraphy, thus creating many memorable masterpieces. In the poetic couplet from the Chien Lu Collection (No. 59, Pl. 31), ductile energy has been achieved through variation in the size and weight of individual characters. Hao described his own method of calligraphy in this way: "When I write I always suspend my wrist, holding my brush with a strength that comes from my heel, travels through my body, and appears at my fingertips. The energy of my whole body is concentrated in the fingers, and then I move my brush. Not half finished, I would be soaking wet with sweat."[61] The couplet exhibits strong fluidity, modulation, and playfulness; it is an example of the possibility for individual invention within the norm of such an ancient script as seal script.

In his early work, Xu Sangeng (1806-1890; No. 25, Pl. 30) followed the Zhe school and was very much influenced by Chen Hongshou (No. 22, Pl. 26) and Zhao Zhichen (No. 23, Pl. 42). Eventually, Xu was able to break away from the increasingly run-of-the-mill work of the followers of the Zhe school. His seal engraving, like his calligraphy (No. 61, Color pl. 9), was inspired by the third-century stele *Tianfa shenchenbei*. In the seals engraved during his late years, he added an elegant curvilinearity to his strokes (No. 25).[62]

In addition to the study of seal-script inscriptions, Zhao Zhiqian (1829-1894) made a diligent study of the stelae and votive inscriptions found on the living rock of Buddhist cave temples at Longmen, in Henan Province, dated to the late fifth-century and early sixth centuries.[63] He engraved the side inscriptions of his seals in a style of calligraphy he learned from these cave temple inscriptions, which were mostly chiseled by anonymous engravers and tended to be rough in workmanship (No. 27, Pl. 32). Often he also engraved pictures on the sides of his seals. His calligraphy is characterized by strong, hard-edged, wedge-shaped strokes with an intricately balanced space between them (No. 60, Color pl. 8). In his calligraphy, he often combined the freedom of running script (*xingshu*) with the monumentality of stele inscription and clerical script. The overall effect is that of an almost effortless inevitability which has been characterized by critics as *mei* (charming) or *shou* (ripe). His seal engraving was inspired by ancient inscriptions found in a variety of sources, including coins from the Warring States period (No. 2, Pl. 10), imperial edicts from the Qin dynasty, mirrors, bricks (Pl. 12; Fig. 2), tile ends (No. 4, Pls. 11, 16), sealing clays from the Han dynasty (No. 51, Pls. 8, 9), and such early stelae as *Tianfa shenchenbei*, *Sisangongshan bei*, and *Shanguoshan bei*. His objective was to reinvigorate his

Pl. 30, (No. 25). Xu Sangeng (1806-1890), **Double-Sided Seal**. Qing dynasty, dated 1885. Qingtian stone. Yi Lei Wang

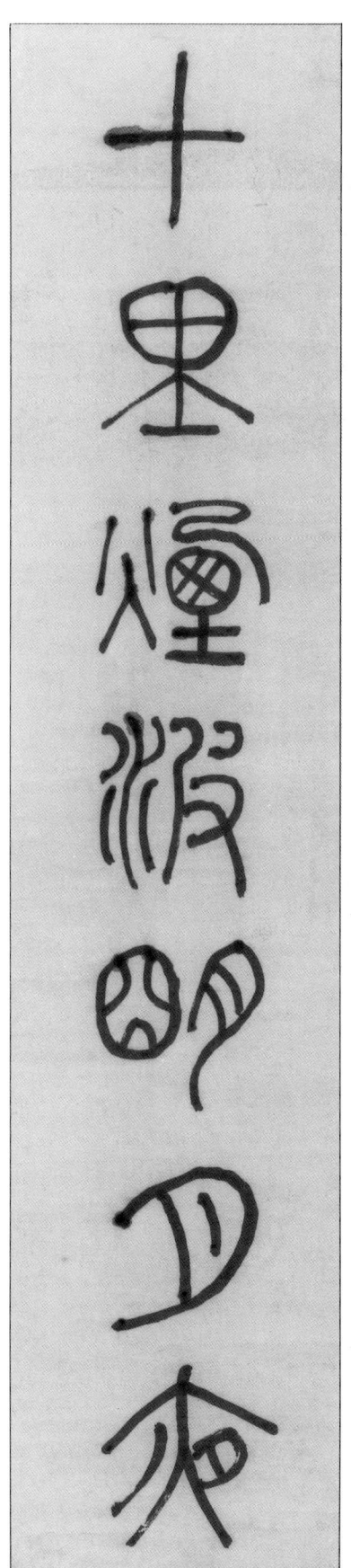

Pl. 31, (No. 59). He Shaoji (1799-1873), **Couplet in Seal Script**. Qing dynasty, 19th c. Pair of hanging scrolls. Chien Lu Collection

Pl. 32, (No. 27). Zhao Zhiqian (1829-1884), **Pair of Seals**. Qing dynasty. Robert Hatfield Ellsworth

seal engraving with the liveliness of strong and fresh brushwork. As he himself put it:

> The beauty in Han bronze seals is not in their varied patterns, but in their powerful simplicity. When studying [this principle and carving it into seals], one relies completely on the power of the wrist. An attribute of rocks is friability, and the strength of the wrist reaches towards the friable parts of a stone. This area of the material responds to the sudden attack of the hand, and falls off. The more unpretentious it is, the older its flavor. When you look at it, it seems ordinary, with nothing striking about it, but it is truly difficult to imitate.... I maintain that one should use the method of penetrating deeply.[64]

Seal Engravers after the Qing Dynasty

The seal engraving of Wu Changshuo (1844-1927; No. 31, Pl. 34; Nos. 32, 33, and 34, Pl. 33; No. 52, Pl. 14) is intimately rooted in his decades of studying bronze and stone inscriptions, particularly the Stone Drum Inscription (No. 62, Pl. 3). Wu Changshuo's interpretations tend to "heighten the interest of the individual characters by unbalancing their component parts and recreate the dynamic tensions of the earlier, more pictographic script. The individual strokes, made with a locked wrist and the arms suspended over the table, show a tautly controlled 'round' brushwork, with a centered, 'hidden' tip."[65] Obvious changes can be observed when comparing his early copies of the Stone Drum Inscription with his later ones. Most apparent is the evolution toward stronger, more blunt brushstrokes, as well as more distorted forms, in which the characters either seem to turn in space or are pulled up on the right side. Wu Changshuo "was capable of great stylistic audacity (unstable equilibriums, deliberate asymmetries, surreptitious regressions of writing towards drawing) which are never obvious and thus infuse his calligraphy with all the more liveliness."[66]

Although he began to paint seriously only after he was about fifty years old, Wu was primarily known for his seal engraving. He exerted a strong influence on twentieth-century Japanese seal engraving, counting the Japanese seal engraver Kawai Senro (1871-1945) among his important pupils. Of the forty volumes in the compendium on Chinese seal engraving, *Chūgoku tenkoku sōkan*, compiled by Kobayashi Toan (b. 1916), a pupil of Kawai Senro, five are devoted to Wu Changshuo.

The seal engraving of Wu Changshuo is characterized by round brushwork and the slow and reserved pace of the seal knife. The structural strength Wu Changshuo learned from his numerous free-hand copies and interpretations of the Stone Drum Inscription (compare No. 1, Pl. 1, with No. 62, Pl. 3) enabled him not only to accomplish great seal engraving but also to reinvigorate Chinese flower painting in the mode of *xieyi*, or writing-out ideas. In the seal *Shiyun shuhua* (No. 52F, Pl. 14), done when he was about fifty-four, the style of the characters was based on the monumentality of Han seals. The seal *Huzhou Anjixian* (No. 52B, Pl. 14), in which the two words *Anji* are reduced in size to occupy one quarter of the available space, recalls the ingenuity

Pl. 34, (No. 31). Wu Changshuo (1844-1927), **Seal**. Dated 1916. Professor and Mrs. Hans H. Frankel

Pl. 33, (from left to right) A: (No. 32). Wu Changshuo (1844-1927), **Seal**. Qing dynasty, dated 1893. Shoushan stone. B: (No. 34). Wu Changshuo (1844-1927), **Seal**. Qing dynasty, dated 1898. Qingtian stone. C: (No. 33). Wu Changshuo (1844-1927), **Seal**. Qing dynasty, dated 1898. Qingtian stone. Yi Lei Wang

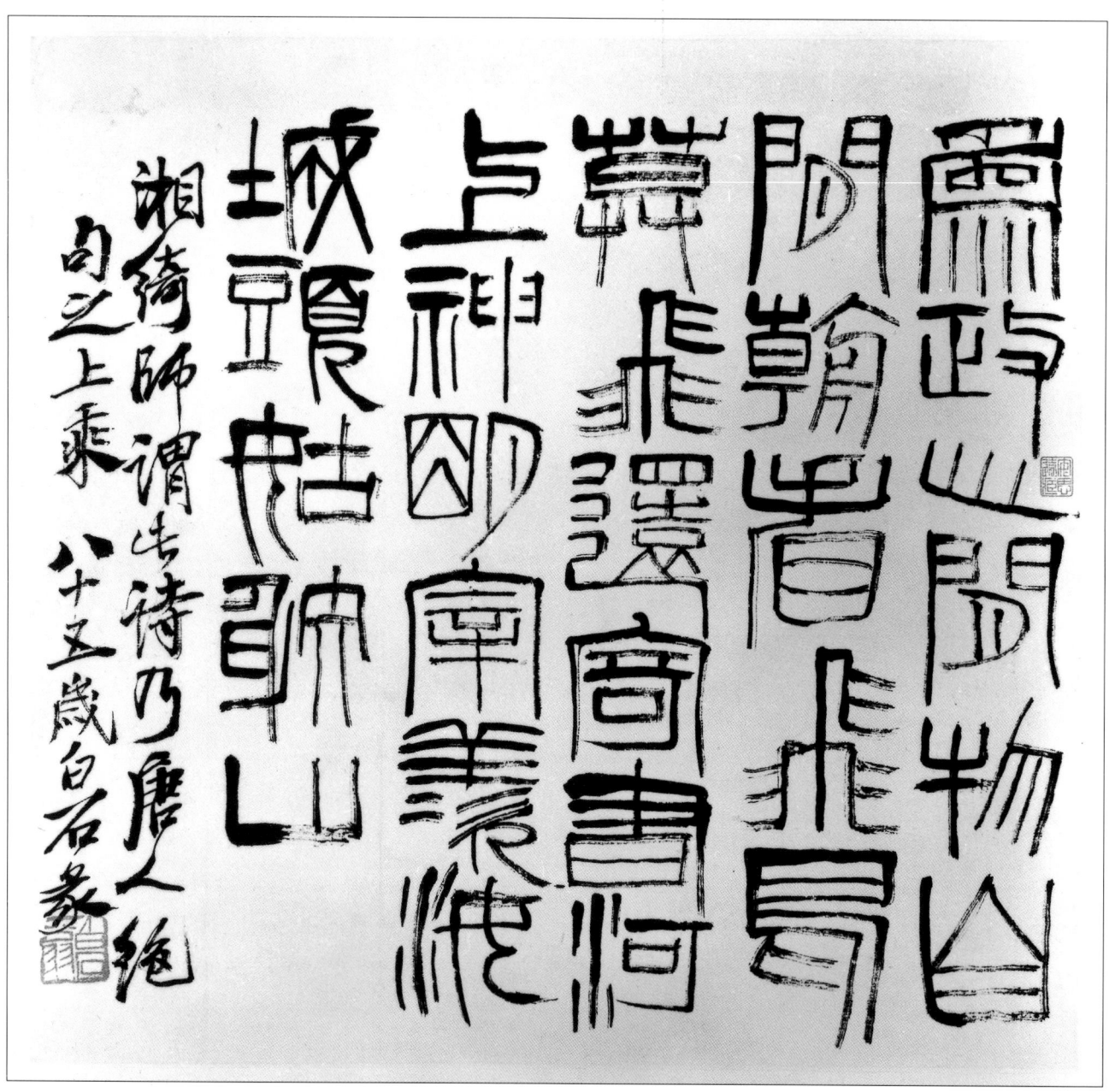

Pl. 35, (No. 64). Qi Baishi (1863-1957), **If You Have a Relaxed Attitude**. Datable to 1948. Album leaf. Robert Hatfield Ellsworth

of molded inscriptions found on Han-dynasty bricks and tile ends. The seal *Meiyi yannian* (No. 52E, Pl. 14), engraved when he was seventy-seven, reveals the strong calligraphic lines derived from decades of study of the Stone Drum Inscription. In the last character, *ting*, from the seal *Soushiting* (No. 52D, Pl. 14), Wu Changshuo elongated the three verticals in the lower part in order to support securely the upper part of the character. Furthermore, *ting* was elongated to balance the two characters on the right. Despite the small number of strokes in the lower part of the seal, the whole seal achieves a dramatic equilibrium, with the sparsity of the lower part balanced against the density of the upper part. Wu Changshuo's seal engraving has strong-

ly influenced many later artists, including Zhao Shi (1875-1933) and Chen Shizeng (1915-1923).[67]

Although best known for his painting, Qi Baishi (1863-1957) has been quoted as saying that he considered his seal engraving a higher achievement than painting.[68] His seal engraving, like his calligraphy and painting, is characterized by a bold, linear beauty and a strong sense of design (No. 36, Pl. 38; No. 53, Pl. 37; No. 64, Pl. 35; No. 65, Pl 36).[69]

Qi's early seal engraving was more conventional and unadventurous, as was his early painting. He began by emulating the seal engravings of Ding Jing and Huang Yi (No. 21) of the Zhe school. Later, he found his main sources of inspiration in the work of Zhao Zhiqian

Pl. 36, (No. 65). Qi Baishi (1863-1957), **Snow Claw**. Datable to 1953. Album leaf. Robert Hatfield Ellsworth

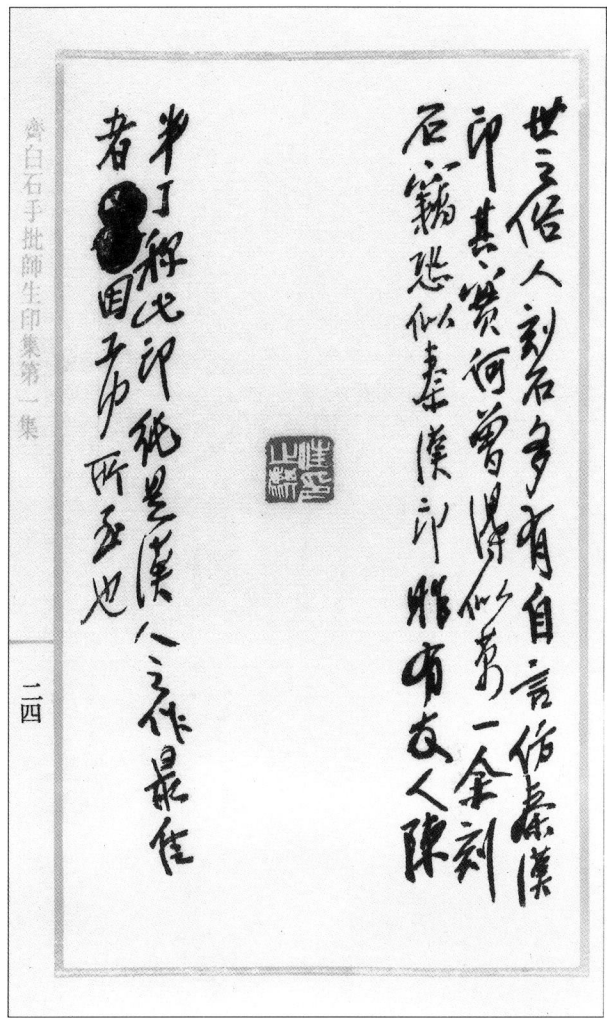

Pl. 37, (No. 53). Qi Baishi (1863-1957) and others, **Qi Baishi shoupi shisheng yinji**. Leaf from a book of seal impressions. Gest Oriental Library and East Asian Collections, Princeton University, New Jersey

(No. 27), as reproduced in Zhao's book of seal impressions entitled *Erjindietang yinpu* (preface by Wu Dacheng dated 1896). He then traced the stylistic origins to the unpretentious inscriptions engraved on bricks by prisoners and to the imperial edicts engraved on weights and measures during the Qin dynasty as well as to the structural configuration of inscriptions in such stelae as the *Sisangongshan bei* and *Tianfa shenchenbei* of the third century. The *Tianfa shenchen* stele (dated 276), with its choppy and angular turn of the strokes, which then taper to a point, exerted a strong influence on the calligraphy and seal engraving of Qi.

Beginning in the 1920s, Qi made a conscientious effort to study the seal engraving and calligraphy of Wu Changshuo, which were to strengthen his own work.[70] Like the seals engraved by Wu, those by Qi retain much of the traces of the pliant brush. They are, however, characterized by a more angular brushwork and a quicker pace of the seal knife than those of Wu. Partly because of his early training as a carpenter and wood engraver and partly because of a strong artistic temperament, Qi Baishi could not satisfy himself with merely emulating Wu Changshuo or any earlier master for that matter. He once commented on his own seal (No. 53, Pl. 37): "Vulgar people often describe their seal engraving as something derived from Qin and Han seals. In fact, they have not learned anything. In my own seals, I am often afraid of looking like Qin and Han."[71]

Qi was very concerned about establishing his own position in art history. He said, "In my seal cutting, when young I made a careful study of the calligraphy of the ancients, then looked for the inner logic of engraving characters. I did not spoil my work by 'imitation,' 'artificial elaboration,' or 'over-polishing,' considering these a waste of energy. When men praised my seals, I smiled; when they ran them down, I smiled."[72] As an indication of Qi's more independent artistic personality, in selecting a phrase for the legend of his seal, he would more often than not use his own words, whereas Wu tended to quote others. Qi also commented, "When I cut seals, I am not bound by old rules and so modern philistines think I follow no tradition. I pity these fellows for their

Pl. 38, (No. 36). Qi Baishi (1863-1957), **Seal**. Dated 1942. Qingtian stone. Yi Lei Wang

stupidity. Can't they understand that we are men just the same as the Qin and Han artists? Can't they understand that we have our special merits, which the men of old would admire too if they could see them?"[73] The dynamic and dramatic visual configuration of his late seals can be seen in an example dated 1942 in the collection of Yi Lei Wang (No. 36, Pl. 38).

Qi's seals have been avidly sought after by his admirers. The contemporary painter Zhu Qizhan, for instance, owns sixty seals by Qi and calls his own studio The Studio of Sixty Seals by Qi Baishi (*Liushi Baishi yin xuan*). Zhu calls himself The Rich Man Who Owns Sixty Seals by Qi Baishi (*Liushi Baishi yin fuweng*).[74]

Although not as well known as Qi, Huang Binhong (1864-1955) can be considered one of the last great literati artists in China.[75] Paintings from his late years have been held in increasingly high regard by serious painters and connoisseurs. However, his paintings can be understood through an examination of his calligraphy and seal engraving (No. 66, Pl. 39). He was not only an avid collector of ancient seals, beginning with the acquisition of a large number of seals originally belonging to the seal collector Wang Qishu (No. 44, Pl. 60), but also a serious student of seal engraving. In fact, he published one of the earliest comprehensive treatises on seal engraving in modern times.[76] In his seal-script calligraphy, Huang tried to infuse a strong archaism, which is also noticeable in the two seals following his signature on a pair of hanging scrolls (No. 66, Pl. 39).[77] His approach to composition in painting, particularly during his late years, can be characterized by the positive use of void and was clearly related to the aesthetic values of seal engraving.[78] Thanks to his many years of practice in seal engraving and calligraphy, he achieved a style of painting that has been characterized as "simple, energetic, classical, and voluminous."[79]

Zhao Shuru, also known as Zhao Shigang (1874-1945), carefully studied the cast and engraved bronze seals of the Han dynasty, as well as inscriptions on ritual bronze vessels, mirrors, and even inscriptions on Buddhist sculpture. He incorporated his visual experience in his seal engraving, much as did Zhao Zhiqian, whom he admired.[80] In contrast to the free and spontaneous style of Wu Changshuo, Zhao Shuru's seal engraving can be characterized as careful and studied. In addition to Han-dynasty inscriptions, he studied bronze inscriptions of the Shang and Zhou dynasties, collected seals, and wrote two books on ancient seals. Both his red-character-impression seals (No. 37) and his seal-script calligraphy were inspired by the small seal script of the Qin dynasty. Other seals, such as the second seal following his signature on a pair of hanging scrolls (No. 63, Pl. 40), were inspired by the archaic seals of the Warring States period.[81]

Zhao Shi (1875-1933) was one of the most important pupils of Wu Changshuo. The archaic and rustic beauty of his seal engravings was most likely derived from designs and inscriptions on sealing clays (No. 38).[82] He even called himself Guni, or Ancient Clays, and Nidaoren, or The Daoist of Clays.

Another important seal engraver of the post-Qing period was Tang Zuishi (1886-1969; No. 39, Pl. 46). Influenced by the Eight Masters of Xiling of the Zhe school, Tang also studied Qin and Han inscriptions on stelae, as well as seals. He was a member of the Xiling Society of Seal Engraving, founded by Wu Changshuo and others in 1904. As a result of his skills in seal engraving, he served in the Mint of the Republic of China.[83]

The works of two modern masters conclude our brief historical survey of seal engraving, though it must be noted that it is an art that is still very much alive today in China. The composition of Qiao Dazhuang's (1892-1948) tend to be unusual, but his strokes are regular and smooth, resulting in a personal and sometimes eccentric style (No. 40A, B). Like many of his predecessors in the nineteenth century, he sought his inspiration in Han-dynasty seals. Deng Sanmu (1898-1963) was a distinguished scholar of the history of Chinese calligraphy as well as a calligrapher in his own right. He studied bronze inscriptions, the Stone Drum Inscription, Han stele inscriptions, and the Wang Xizhi (321-379) tradition of calligraphy. His seal engraving was based on a

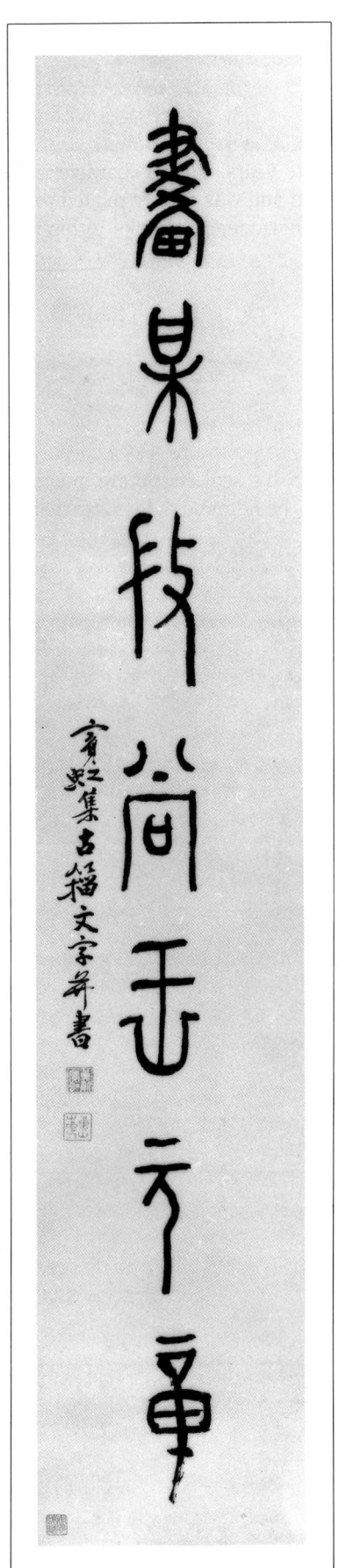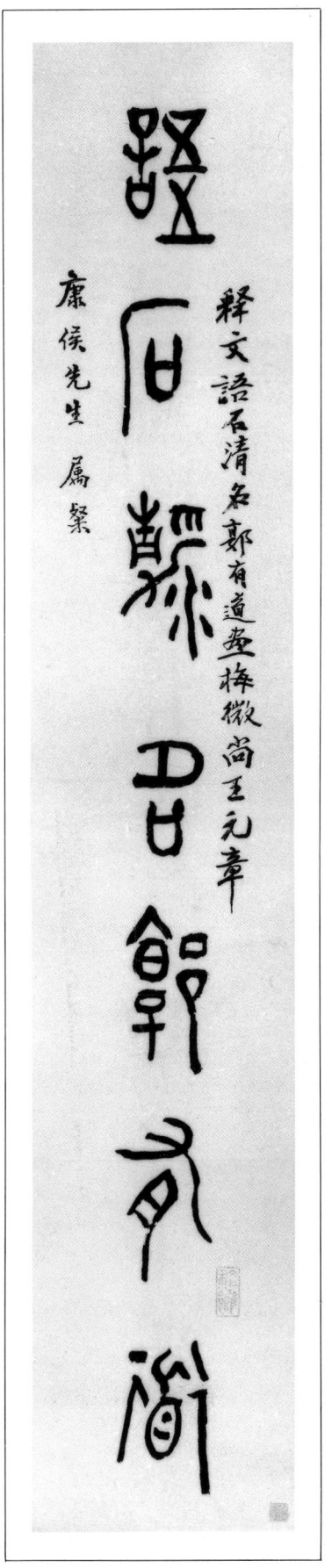

Pl. 39, (No. 66). Huang Binhong (1864-1955), **In Describing Rocks**.
Pair of hanging scrolls. Robert Hatfield Ellsworth

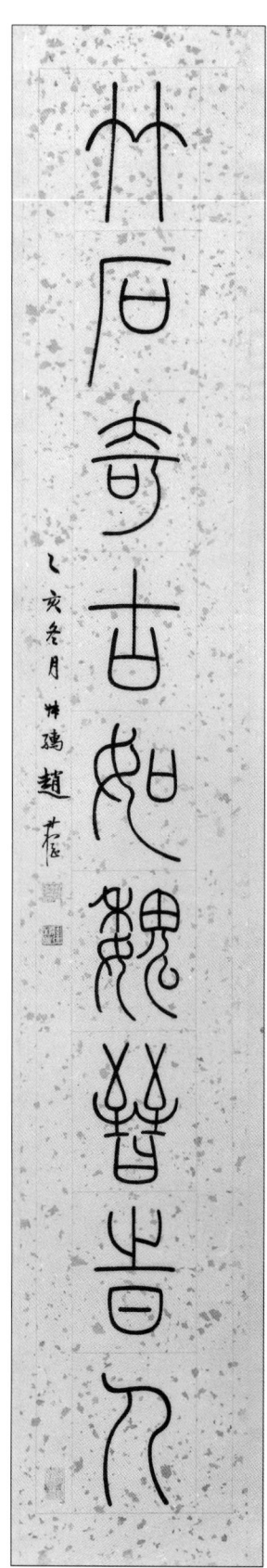

Pl. 40, (No. 63). Zhao Shuru (1874-1945), **Calligraphy in Seal Script**. Dated 1935. Pair of hanging scrolls. Robert Hatfield Ellsworth

lifetime study of inscriptions on sealing clays, pottery, and bricks. A follower of Zhao Shi (Zhao Guni; No. 38) in seal engraving, he paid much attention to the configuration of the script as well as to the composition of the whole legend (No. 41, Pl. 43). His treatise on seal engraving, *Zhuankexue*, first published in 1979, has become one of the most popular textbooks on the subject.[84]

SOME AESTHETIC ASPECTS OF THE ART OF SEAL ENGRAVING

The late-sixteenth-century author Zhou Gongjin compared seal engraving to other art forms: "Prose, poetry, calligraphy, painting—these are the same as seal engraving."[85] Chen Wanyan, in his preface to the *Xueshantang yinpu* compiled by Zhang Hao (1633), saw no difference between seal engraving and painting: "The literati are engaged in seal engraving as play, just as they are engaged in painting where the emotions of mountains and the ideas of water are merely vehicles of their own feelings."[86]

The canons developed for seal engraving are similar to those long used for calligraphy and painting. For example, according to the *Moyin chuandeng* compiled by Ye Erkuan of the Qing dynasty (1874), there are Six Canons (*liufa*) in seal engraving: first, a seal must display rhythmic vitality or consonance; second, the knife must be employed to achieve a flavor of antiquity and a sense of energy; third, a seal must have a well-balanced composition; fourth, the seal script must be correctly constructed and elegant; fifth, the engraving must adhere to the brushwork; sixth, a seal must not be vulgar. Furthermore, Ye Erkuan listed Six Essentials (*liuyao*): first, a seal must display the flavor of learning; second, a seal must have a sense of antiquity, with intentional clumsiness but at the same time liveliness; third, the composition must reflect the interaction of tension and equilibrium; fourth, the ancient methods must be followed; fifth, the bone and the flesh of the lines must balance each other; six, the layout of columns and spacing must be carefully planned. Finally, he listed the Six Merits (*liuchang*) of a seal: first, elegance in clumsiness; second, strength in delicacy; third, rhythm in empty space; fourth, forcefulness in seeming weakness; fifth, reasonableness in unreasonableness; sixth, softness in roughness.[87]

Furthermore, the seventeenth-century painter Gao Fu praised the unique qualities of seal engraving as distinguished from other art forms:

> The calligraphy of Li Si and Cheng Miao [of the Qin dynasty] could be inscribed on the towering mountain cliffs, but could not be aesthetic objects on the table. The poetry of Li Bo and Du Fu could describe mist and cloud, but could not comfort the tiny fingers. It is only in seal engraving that one can sum up a thousand words in a few characters, reduce ten feet to

half a jade tablet, include all kinds of inscriptions from stone and metal monuments, and make possible the same pleasure as poetry and music.[88]

This statement is particularly appropriate to the type of seals that began to be favored by the literati in the sixteenth century, namely the leisure seal (*xianzhang*). The leisure seals usually contain phrases that are either literary allusions or expressive of the artists' or the recipients' aspirations or personalities. For example, a favorite seal used by the seventeenth-century artist Shitao was *Soujin Qifeng dacaogao* (Search out strange peaks and make sketches of them).[89] The emphasis on literary allusions and expressive content in seals rather then merely the identification of personal names and studio names suggests the increasing independence of seal engraving as an aesthetic pursuit starting with the sixteenth century.

Also beginning in the sixteenth century, seal engravers added inscriptions to the sides of the seal itself. These side inscriptions (*biankuan*) often contain both the signature of the seal engraver and a short comment in prose or poetry, thus serving the same function as inscriptions or colophons on a painting and enhancing the literary flavor of the art of seal engraving.

In his preface to Hu Yuecong's *Yincun chuji* of 1661 (No. 43, Color pl. 3), the late-Ming-dynasty writer Wu Qi said of the compositional aspects of seal engraving:

> Although a seal is small, no longer than a finger, and no larger than two square inches, it contains development and structure and, in its sweep and profundity, can be as satisfactory as a fine work of literary art. Furthermore, it can make oneself feel leisurely and calm, but it can also suddenly stir up emotions sometimes as [strong as] dragons and sometimes as [convoluted as] snakes; it cannot be regarded merely as a literary composition.[90]

This statement suggests that, although seals—particularly those containing literary allusions or extensive expressive phrases—have a strong literary content, they are also objects of visual art. To appreciate them is to appreciate the two-dimensional compositions or designs of both the seals themselves and the impressions they make on paper or silk. Many compositional schemes peculiar to the small dimensions of a seal's legend can be distinguished and classified as mentioned above.

Although it is a form of Chinese calligraphy, seal engraving has special qualities that are absent from calligraphy written with a soft brush and achieved only with the use of a knife incising a hard surface. Depending on the type of knife used and the technique of cutting, a variety of visual effects can be achieved for various expressive purposes. For example, Wu Changshuo usually employed a knife with a thick and blunt cutting edge in order to achieve an

Pl. 41, (No. 21). Huang Yi (1744-1802), **Seal**. Qing dynasty, dated 1777. Qingtian stone. Yi Lei Wang

Pl. 42, (No. 23). Zhao Zhichen (1781-1852), **Seal**. Qing dynasty, dated 1827. Qingtian stone. Yi Lei Wang

archaistic flavor in his seals.

Furthermore, the tactile quality of the stones used for seals is an important aspect of the art of seal engraving. Like jades, the various kinds of stone were avenues for expressing the different tastes of the artists. Most commonly used were soft soapstones, including the Qingtian stone, a greenish serpentine found in Qingtian,

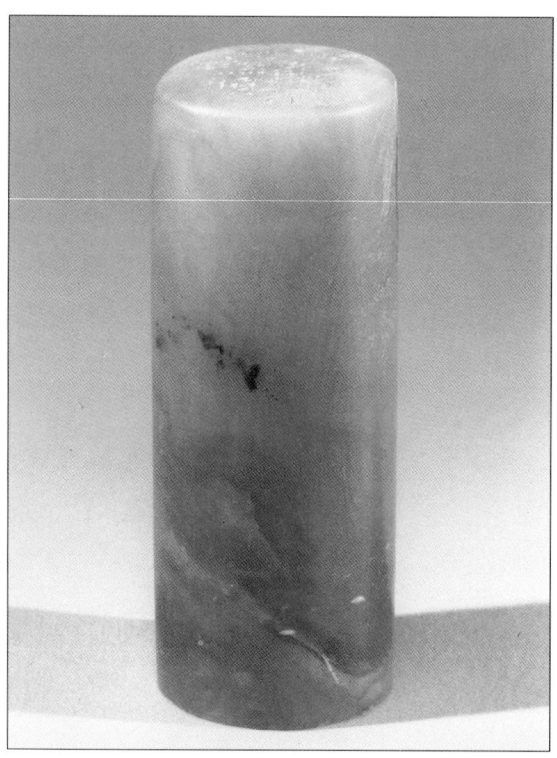

Pl. 43, (No. 41). Deng Sanmu, **Seal**. Dated 1938. Shoushan stone. Yi Lei Wang

Pl. 44, (No. 38). Zhao Guni (1875-1933), **Seal**. Dated 1929. Shoushan stone. Yi Lei Wang

Pl. 45, (No. 37). Zhao Shuru (1874-1945), **Seal**. Dated 1917. Shoushan stone. Yi Lei Wang

Pl. 46, (No. 39). Tang Zuishi (1886-1969), **Seal**. Dated 1947. Shoushan stone. Yi Lei Wang

Zhejiang Province (No. 21, Pl. 41; No. 23, Pl. 42; No. 33 and 34, Pl. 33; No. 36, Pl. 38). Another major type is the Shoushan stone, a serpentine of white, brown, red, and other colors, quarried near Fuzhou, Fujian Province (No. 20, Pl. 48; No. 22, Pl. 26; No. 24, Pl. 29; No. 32, Pl. 33; No. 37, Pl. 45; No. 38, Pl. 44; No. 39, Pl. 46; No. 41, Pl. 43).

"White Hibiscus" is one of the most treasured of Shoushan stones (No. 31, Pl. 34; No. 35, Pl. 49; No. 40, Pl. 47).

The combination of calligraphy, literature, engraving, and tactile experience makes Chinese seal engraving a fascinating art that is practiced by an increasing

Pl. 47, (No. 40). Qiao Dazhuang (1892-1948), **Pair of Seals**. Shoushan stone, "white hibiscus" type. Wang Fang-yu and Sum Wai Wang

Pl. 48, (No. 20). Zhou Bin (active late 17th c.), **Fisherman**. Qing dynasty. Shoushan stone. Wang Fang-yu and Sum Wai Wang

number of Chinese artists. Furthermore, the study of seal engraving is an important aspect of the connoisseurship of Chinese calligraphy and painting.

As recently as the 1970s, the painter Chen Zizhuang (1913-1976) admitted that his own painting was very much influenced by such principles of seal engraving as *yinyang* and the mutual response of void and substance which were first laid down by Wu Qiuyan (14th c.) in his pioneering work on seal engraving, *Sanshiwuju* (*Thirty-five Principles*).[91]

Compositional Considerations in Seal Engraving

One of the most salient features of a seal engraving is its small size. For the cultured literati, smallness is no detraction. What Shen Fu (1763-1808) in his *Fusheng liuji* said of the principles in designing gardens can be said of seal engraving: "To show the small in the big, and the big in the small."[92] The appreciation of smallness is also evident in Zheng Xie's (1693-1765) comment on his bamboo and rock garden:

> In front of my tiny room is a small yard in which stand several bamboo and a few rocks in the shapes of bamboo shoots. Since it is not large, it requires little money. It has the sound of wind and rain, shadows thrown by the sun and moon, and a cordial atmosphere in which to drink or write poetry, and there are friends about to keep me company when I am relaxing or feeling low.... Some people spend vast amounts building gardens and pavilions, but then travel far and wide as officials and cannot return to enjoy them. I cannot afford the time to travel to the great mountains and rivers. I would rather know the happiness of living in this small room, which will last for many years and will always be stimulating. Contemplating these picturesque surroundings, I do not find it difficult to condense everything and hide it away in some secret place or to expand it to fill the whole world.[93]

Like Zheng Xie's small garden, seal engraving creates a microcosm in which the virtual forces or gestures of the world could be captured. Small is beautiful.

Another principle of garden design mentioned by Shen Fu is also quite significant for seal engraving: "To see substance in void and to see void in substance."[94] In seal engraving, the interaction of void (emptiness or space) and substance (strokes or characters) is of primary importance. One of the most frequently mentioned desiderata is to achieve the effects of being "spacious enough to walk a horse in" (*shukezouma*), as in a seal engraved by Wu Changshuo (No. 33), and being "so crowded that not even a breath of air could pass through" (*mibutongfeng*) or "not even a needle could pass through" (*miburongzhen*), as in the seal engraved by Tang Zuishi (No. 39).

This conception of the seal (and seal impression) as a microcosm is deeply rooted in philosophical Daoism. For example, Chapter 11 of *Daodejing* maintains:

> We put thirty spokes together and call
>   it a wheel;
> But it is on the space where there is nothing
>   that the utility of the wheel depends.
> We turn clay to make a vessel;
> But it is on the space where there is nothing
>   that the utility of the vessel depends.
> We pierce doors and windows to make a house;
> And it is on these spaces where there is nothing
>   that the utility of the house depends.
> Therefore, just as we take advantage of what is,
>   we should recognize the utility of what
>   is not.[95]

A seal is a self-sufficient world that has its own dynamics. The dynamics are similar to those embodied in the well-known ancient Chinese emblem called *Taijitu*, or the Diagram of the Primordial Unity (Fig. 4). In the *Taijitu*, the lighter half, *yang*, represents that which is active or masculine, and the darker half, *yin*, that which is passive or feminine. The sigmoid line bisecting the circle represents the movement or play of forces around the unchanging center.

Ideally, then, the visual image of a seal (and its impression) should be similar to that of a piece of calligraphy or a painting in which a whole "world" (*jingjie*) is created by the artist. The artist must, as Shitao described it in Chapter 5 of his *Huayulu*:

> Create embryonic and structured form, openness and closeness, substance and function, forms and power, bowing and standing, squatting and leaping, that which hides in waters or soars into the clouds, teetering cliffs, vastness, irregular peaks, monumental and awesome heights, odd peaks and dangerous precipices.[96]

Another way to understand seal engraving as a calligraphic art is through the concept of *shi*, momentum or gesture, a term used by many early Chinese theorists of art and literature, including Cai Yong. As Martin Powers has pointed out recently, *shi* is intimately related to other key critical terms, such as *tai* and *qi*.[97] It is also appropriate to understand seal engraving as a calligraphic art through what John Hay has described as human body structure:

> It is immediately effective to ask someone, in their first meeting with [Chinese] calligraphy, to look at the characters as though they were a body structure—as supporting skeletal struc-

Fig. 4. **Taijitu** (Diagram of Primordial Unity)

tures made beautiful with flesh, and strong with muscle and sinew—to suggest they grasp kinesthetically the implications of movement, so that they can perceive the tensions and balance within the writing through these same functions within their body.[98]

Like a painting or a piece of calligraphy, then, a seal as a two-dimensional composition must be approached in terms of the endless varieties and interactions of tension and resolution, symmetry and asymmetry, balance and instability, unity and fragmentation, economy and intricacy, consistency and variation, singularity and juxtaposition, positive and negative, contrast and harmony, and so forth.[99]

Side Inscriptions *(biankuan)*

Although inscriptions on the sides of the seals appeared on official seals in the Tang dynasty, it was during the late Ming period that seal engravers began to add personal or studio names, phrases, poems, and even short prose. Often artists other than the seal engravers would add colophons to the sides of the seal as if adding a colophon to a piece of calligraphy and painting (see, for example No. 21, Pl. 41).

In addition to its visual effect and tactile quality on the side of a seal, the side inscription was often appreciated by the literati in the form of rubbings collected, together with seal impressions, in a seal book. No doubt this practice was related to the literati appreciation of rubbings as works of art. The earliest extant rubbing is dated to the mid-seventh century, although rubbings of engraved texts are known to have existed as early as the Six Dynasties period.[100] James C. Y. Watt has observed that "a large proportion of late Ming literature on connoisseurship was devoted to rubbings, and the meticulous attention and intense connoisseurship lavished on stone inscriptions sharpened the eye of the scholar/collector to an extraordinary degree."[101]

The side inscription usually appears on the left side of the seal when the seal is held in the correct position for making an impression. When the inscription was too long, however, the convention was to inscribe it so that it terminated on the left side of the seal. Therefore, if a side inscription occupies three sides of the seal, it must begin on the right side, continue to the front or side facing the user, and terminate on the left side of the stone. The only exception is an inscription that occupies more space than the four sides of a seal. In that case, the inscription terminates at the top of the seal.

Perhaps in order to give prominence to the legend, which is usually engraved in seal script or other ancient script forms, the side inscription was usually engraved in later scripts such as clerical script, regular script, or even cursive script. A side inscription can be appreciated for the way in which the knife was used and for the brushwork that lies behind the engraved lines as well as for the composition of individual characters and the relationships between characters.

Although pictorial side inscriptions occur occasionally, as on seals engraved by Zhao Zhiqian, most side inscriptions consist of characters. Often viewed in the form of rubbings (see below), the side inscriptions on seals must be judged according to the same criteria as Chinese calligraphy in regard to their compositions as a whole, the construction of individual characters, and individual strokes. When the main text of the side inscription is a poem or a short passage of prose, it must also be judged as a literary work of art.

Stones for Seal Engraving

Although many different kinds of material have been used for seals, by far the most favored material for seal engraving, particularly since the Yuan dynasty, has been soapstone, or more precisely, pyrophyllite, a hydrous aluminum silicate resembling talc. Soft soapstone was favored by the literati because it was easier for them to engrave. Earlier, the literati simply wrote out the legend and asked a professional artisan-engraver to do the actual cutting.

The literati had long been fascinated by stones. Mi Fu (1051-1107) stands out as the most eccentric example. It is said that, wearing his official robe and carrying his tablet of office, he bowed deeply before a stone and addressed it as his "Elder Brother." The lore of stones has been perpetuated in many literary compositions. One example is the "Song of Shoushan Stones for

Engraving Seals," written by the seventeenth-century painter Mei Qing (1623-1697):

> Who said Mi Fu was mad?
> Yes, he greeted rocks and bowed to them,
>   but his fame spread.
> Who said Jia Xian was eccentric?
> Yes, he boiled stones to appease his hunger,
>   but I love him for it.
> Unusual things and unusual persons
>   are often bedfellows—
> Unplanned, yet, I dare say, arranged by gods.
> Heaven has willed that beauty should
>   adorn the kingdom,
> So that the Si and the Fan could produce
>   variegated stones.
> Of peerless beauty are Qingtian and Jiudong;
> Bright and shimmering are Bingjian
>   and Yunao;
> Recently Shoushan stones outshine them all
> With many colors and the quality of jade.
>
> Is it true that Nüwa, while mending the sky,
> Pried loose these precious stones, the creams
>   of heaven?
> Thunder and storm came like the rising
>   of dragons;
> Then the earth split, and lo!
> Out poured the glittering gems—
> Tangerine-yellow, wax-white, mercuric-fat-red,
> Lufu, Aiye—oh, wonder of wonders!
> Then a lion is carved or a tiger or
>   a kneeling tortoise;
> When the *zhuanshu* script is inscribed
>   one is reminded of Li Si.
> My adventurous friend Lu Zi went to the
>   Eastern Sea
> And from there sent me four tablets of stone.
> Even now iridescence radiates from my hands
> And I sing as if drunken; my true heart sings.
> Ask me, if you please, what my great love is.
> I have a room called Stone-Worship Studio.[102]

Chinese stone lore abounds with reverence for jade which has long been a material with important religious, cultural, and moral significance. Furthermore, the use of rocks in Chinese gardens have long embodied Chinese aesthetic criteria of the highest order.[103] Thus it was no surprise that soapstones, the material favored by the literati for engraving seals, eventually became part of the Chinese lore of the rock.

One of the most favored soapstones is Shoushan stone—the subject of Mei Qing's poem—which comes from Shoushan, Fujian Province. The colors of Shoushan stone are variegated; the best-known types are the white-colored *tianbai* and the yellowish orange *tianhuang*; other varieties range in color from light green to dark brown and black. However, it is their fine-

Pl. 49, (No. 35). Qi Baishi (1863-1957), **Seal**. Shoushan stone, "white hibiscus" type. Wang Fang-yu and Sum Wai Wang

Pl. 50, (No. 19). **Buddhist Seal**. Ming dynasty (1368-1644). Bronze. Field Museum of Natural History, Chicago; no. 117073, (neg. no. A111834)

grained appearance and subtle surface finish, smooth and delicate to the touch that have appealed most to the literati beginning in the late Ming period. Soapstone has also commanded high regard from the literati because their colors and tactile qualities are comparable to those of jade. The popularity of yellow jade during the Yuan, Ming, and Qing dynasties probably accounted for the popularity of *tianhuang* (No. 26, Color pl. 5).[104] A seal engraved by Qi Baishi on a stone carved centuries earlier by Zhou Bin (active ca. late seventeenth century) is a good example of *baifurong*, or "white hibiscus," a type of Shoushan stone treasured for its translucent cream white color; it is now in the collection of Wang Fang-yu (No. 35, Pl. 49).

Another type of stone is Qingtian stone, named for its place of origin in Zhejiang Province. Like Shoushan stone, it is a pyrophyllite. The most common ones are greenish in color, but others are brownish, purplish, and even black.

A third type of pyrophyllite comes from Changhua, Zhejiang Province. The best-known variety is called *jixue*, or chicken-blood, treasured for its dramatic mottled red inclusions. Other stones from many parts of China as well as Korea and Thailand are also used.

Apart from soft stones, materials for seals include bronze (No. 11, Pl. 18; No. 14, Color pl. 1; No. 15, Pl. 21; No. 16, Color Pl. 2; No. 17, Pl. 22; No. 18, Pl. 23; No. 19, Pl. 50), gold, silver (No. 5, Pl. 15), iron, jade (No. 30, Pl. 52; Nos. 7, 8, 9, and 10, Pl. 19), crystal, wood, bamboo roots, fruit seeds, roots of old plum-trees, horn, ivory (No. 28, Color pl. 4, Pl. 51), bones, pottery, porcelain, and so forth.

Tools for Seal Engraving of Soapstones

The most important tool of seal engraving is the knife (No. 68, Pl. 53). Although often called the "iron brush," or *tiebi*, the modern seal engraver's knife is generally made from tempered steel. It is approximately 15 centimeters long, with a blade at both ends slanted at

Pl. 51, (No. 28). Huang Wenhan (active late 19th c.), **Double-Sided Seal**. Qing dynasty, dated 1881. Ivory. Dr. Paul Singer

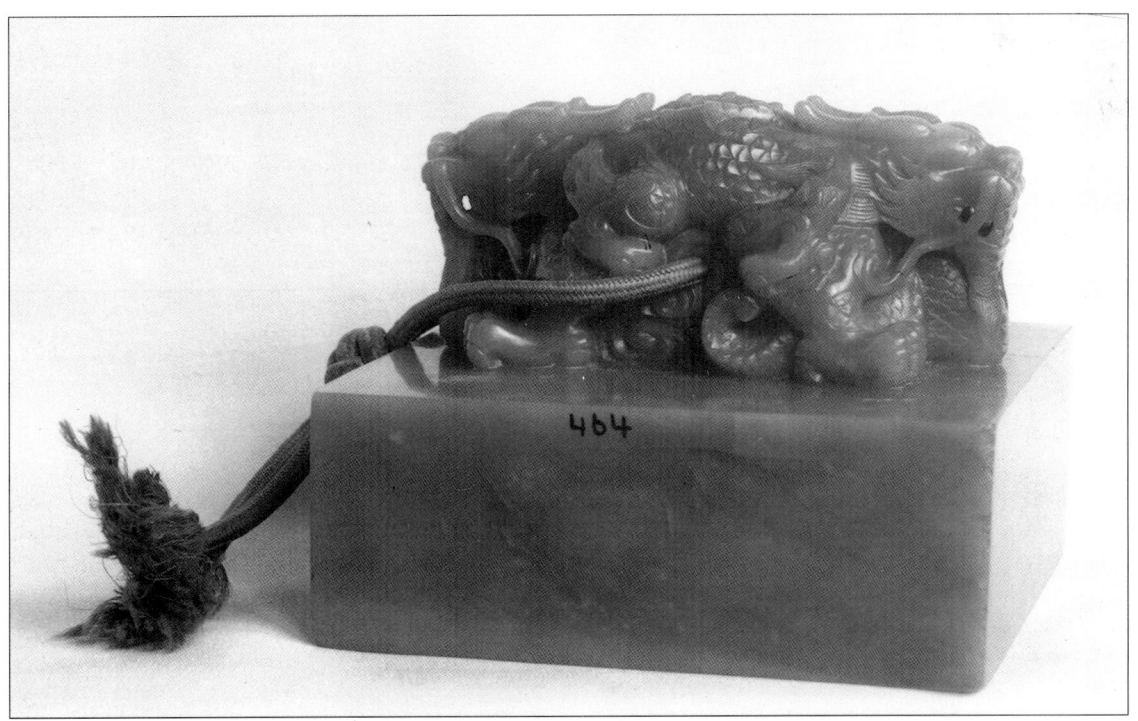

Pl. 52, (No. 30). **Seal with Double Dragon**. Qing dynasty (1644-1912). Nephrite. The Metropolitan Museum of Art, New York; Gift of Heber R. Bishop, 1902

about 30 degrees. In the middle it has a grip, about 10 centimeters in length, longer than the sleeve of a typical modern scriber, or engraving knife; the grip is usually made of tightly rolled silk, cotton, or rattan string to prevent the knife from slipping in the hand. Only a few knives are needed, with tips ranging in width from 1 to 5 millimeters.

Sandpaper good for wet-sanding is needed to prepare the stone. Three grades should be available for preparing different surfaces: rough, medium, and polished.

A clamp that consists of a number of wooden wedges of varying sizes for securing the stone being engraved is sometimes needed (No. 69, Pl. 54). However, true to the literati aversion to any craft or skill that smacks of professionalism, most seal engravers prefer to hold the stone with one hand while wielding the knife with the other.

Three ways of holding the knife can be distinguished, according to the contemporary seal engraver Wang Beiyue (b. 1926), who studied under He Kongcai, a pupil of Qi Baishi:[105]

1. Gripping the middle of the knife with five fingers as if to make a fist, with the tip of the knife coming from under the little finger. The advantage of this method is that it allows a much stronger grip of the knife, ideal for engraving seal legends that are spontaneous and quick in pace. Qi Baishi favored this method.

2. Similar to holding the brush for calligraphy, the second method involves grasping the grip in the middle of the knife between the thumb and the index, middle, and ring fingers, with the little finger in support. The upper phalange of the thumb presses on the left side of the knife. The top of the index finger presses on the right side of the knife; part of the middle grip of the knife lies on the middle phalange of the index finger. The top of the middle finger hooks around the anterior side of the knife. The fingernail and some of the flesh of the ring finger backs onto the posterior side of the knife. Finally, the little finger is held close behind the ring finger, supporting it and giving added firmness to the knife. The advantage of this method is that it gives the engraver more flexibility in the use of the knife. The knife is generally held in a position 45 degree away from the engraver. This was the most commonly used method for many of the masters of the Zhe (Zhejiang) and the Hui or Wan (Anhui) schools of seal engraving. Wu Changshuo also liked to use this method.

3. The third method for holding the knife is very similar to the way a modern fountain pen or ballpoint pen is held. The thumb, index finger, and middle finger hold the middle grip of the knife and push the tip either away from the engraver or horizontally, parallel to the position of the engraver.

Additionally, there are two different ways of placing the tip (or, more precisely, the slanted blade) of the

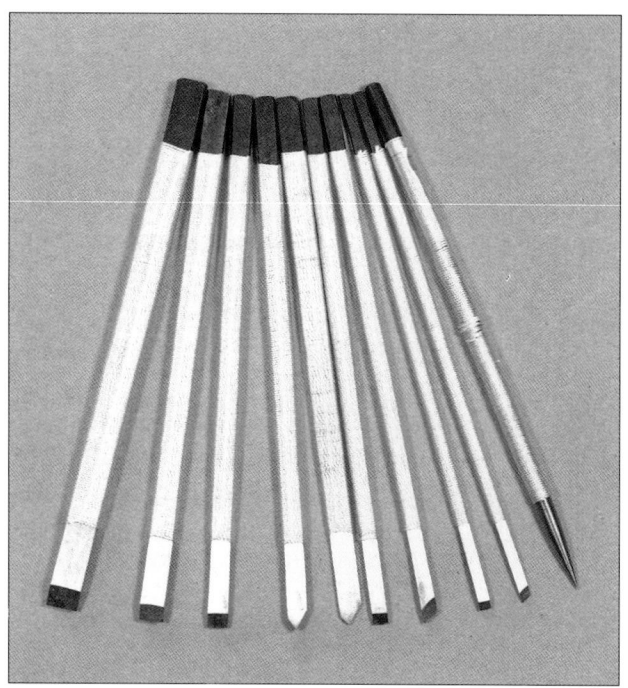

Pl. 53, (No. 68). **Set of Seal-Engraving Knives**. 20th c. Private Collection.

Pl. 54, (No. 69). **Seal Clamp**. 20th c. Private Collection.

knife. According to one method, the knife is held almost perpendicularly with 80 percent of the knife's tip touching the stone. The position parallels that of the brush in calligraphy in that it achieves the effect of *zhongfeng*, or "tip in the middle of the brush." The second method is comparable to the oblique brush position by achieving the effect of *cefeng*, or "oblique tip," as it is referred to in calligraphy. The knife is held toward either the left or the right at 75 degrees; only one end of the tip of the knife touches the stone, thereby producing a broader indention than achieved through the other method.

Over the centuries, many more ways of holding the knife have been espoused, but the three described

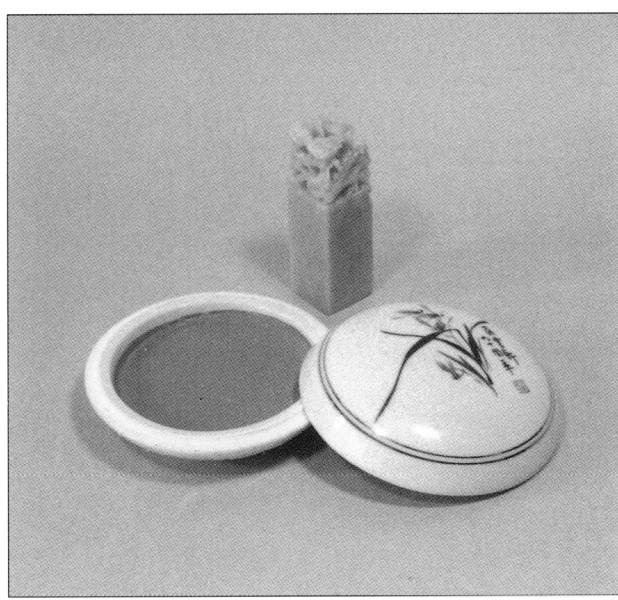

Pl. 55, (No. 67). **Seal Paste and Seal-Paste Box**. 20th c. Private Collection.

Pl. 56, (No. 70). **Seal Paste Box**. Qing dynasty (1644-1912). Nephrite. The Metropolitan Museum of Art, New York; Gift of Heber R. Bishop, 1902

that determine the outcome of the seal.

There are two ways of preparing the design to be engraved. In most cases, particularly for beginners, the legend is designed and written with a brush on a piece of thin, translucent paper. Then the paper is turned over to reveal the design in reverse; the reversed design can then be copied with a brush onto the surface of the stone before one begins to engrave. Another method is to design and write the legend on a piece of paper that is water-tolerant. The piece of paper is made wet with water, and the written design placed on the stone surface. Slight pressure with the fingernails is used to transfer the design onto the stone surface. Finally, one removes the paper from the stone and begins to engrave.

Although the side inscription can be written first on the stone and then engraved, in most cases it has been engraved directly. The two methods of using the knife for engraving the legend described above, namely pushing forward and pushing downward, are also used in engraving the side inscription. A third method is to use a sharp, pointed scriber, particularly for cursive script, which demands a much faster pace in execution.

Impressing the Seal

Unlike a piece of calligraphy or a painting, a seal is ultimately to be read through its impression onto the surface of paper or silk. To obtain a good impression of a seal's legend, a quality vermilion seal paste is used. A pad of silk fibers, stored in a fine porcelain or jade container (No. 70, Pl. 56), is saturated with a mixture of punk of moxa, oil, vermilion powder, and other precious materials. The resulting paste has a thick and plastic texture (No. 67, Pl. 55). In addition, its application to a piece of calligraphy or a painting on paper or silk involves the successful transfer of the vermilion onto the fibers.

Rubbings can be made of the side inscription in the same manner as rubbings from wood blocks, stelae, and bronze vessels. In general, two kinds of rubbing have been distinguished. One is called *wujinta*, or "black-gold rubbing," and the other, *chanyita*, or "cicada-wing rubbing."[106] The latter refers to a lightly inked rubbing, used more often for a short inscription or for a seal with a pictorial image in low relief on its sides, and the former refers to a rubbing made with much darker ink, giving it a dark and shining appearance.

Books of Seals and Seal Impressions (*Yinpu*)

The seal impression can also be appreciated for its own sake by being bound into a book of seal impressions, or *yinpu*. Such books originated in the Tang dynasty as records of seals and seal impressions and became more

above are the most common. Again, only two ways of using the knife can be distinguished even if many others have been proffered. One is to push the knife forward while holding the tip obliquely as described above; the other is to push the knife downward as it is pushed slightly forward. Ultimately, it is the engraver's mastery of the techniques of using the knife as well as the level of his mastery of calligraphy

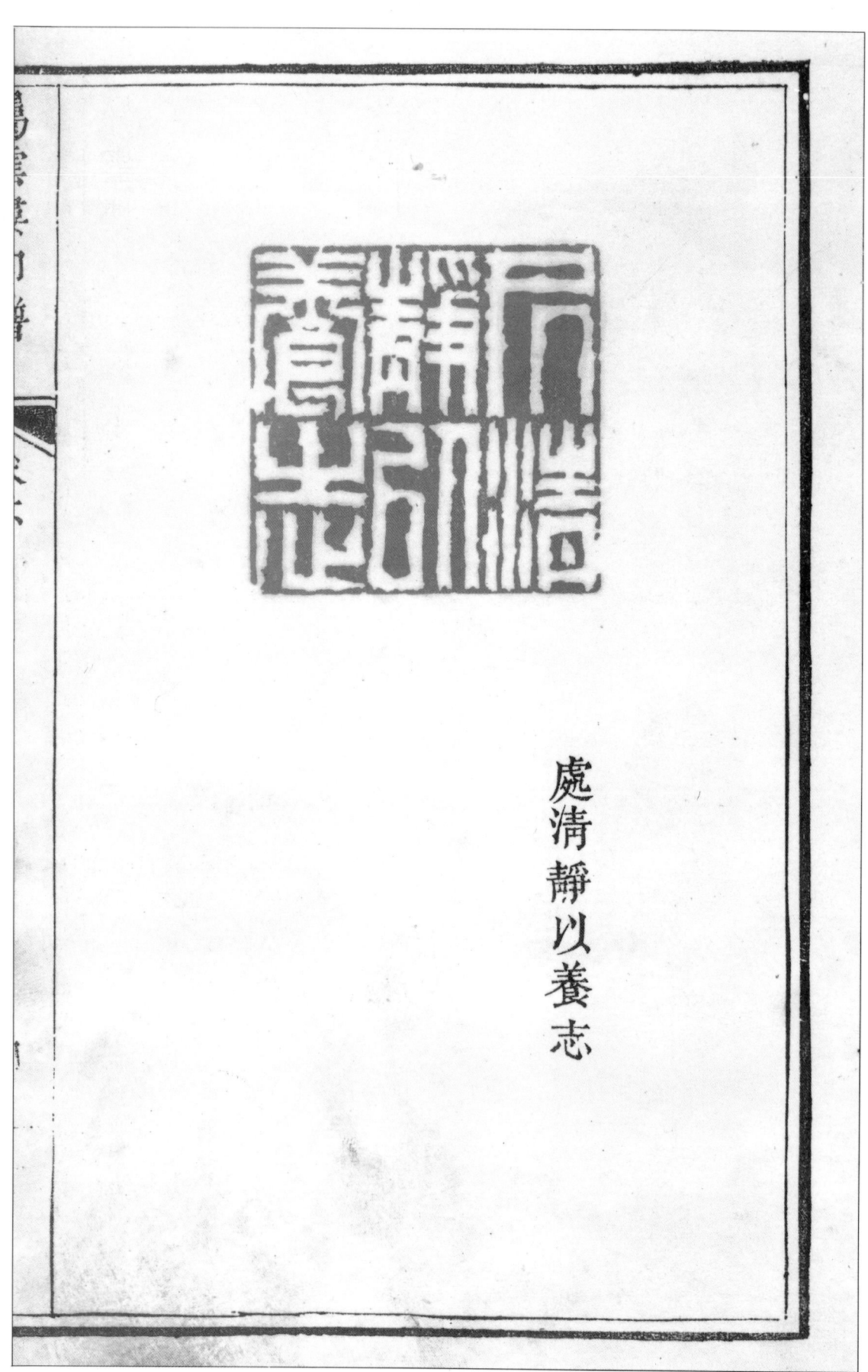

Pl. 57, (No. 45). Chen Lian (1730-1778), **Shuyunlou yinpu**.
Qing dynasty, dated 1765. Two leaves from a woodblock
printed book of seal impressions. Guanhai Lou Collection

屬雲樓印譜卷下

雲間
陳　鍊在專鐵筆
汪永楷皆木校訂

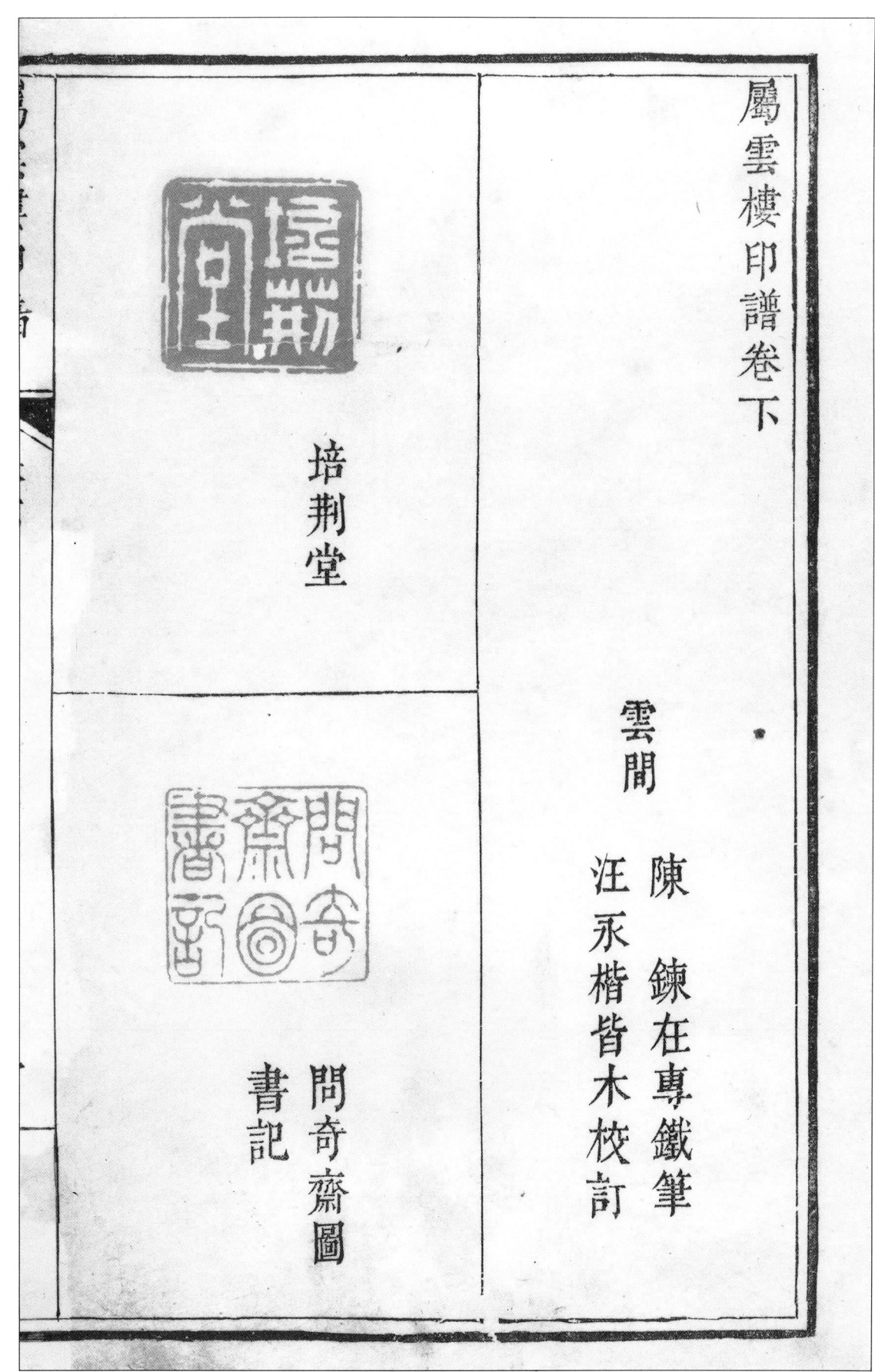

培荊堂

問奇齋圖書記

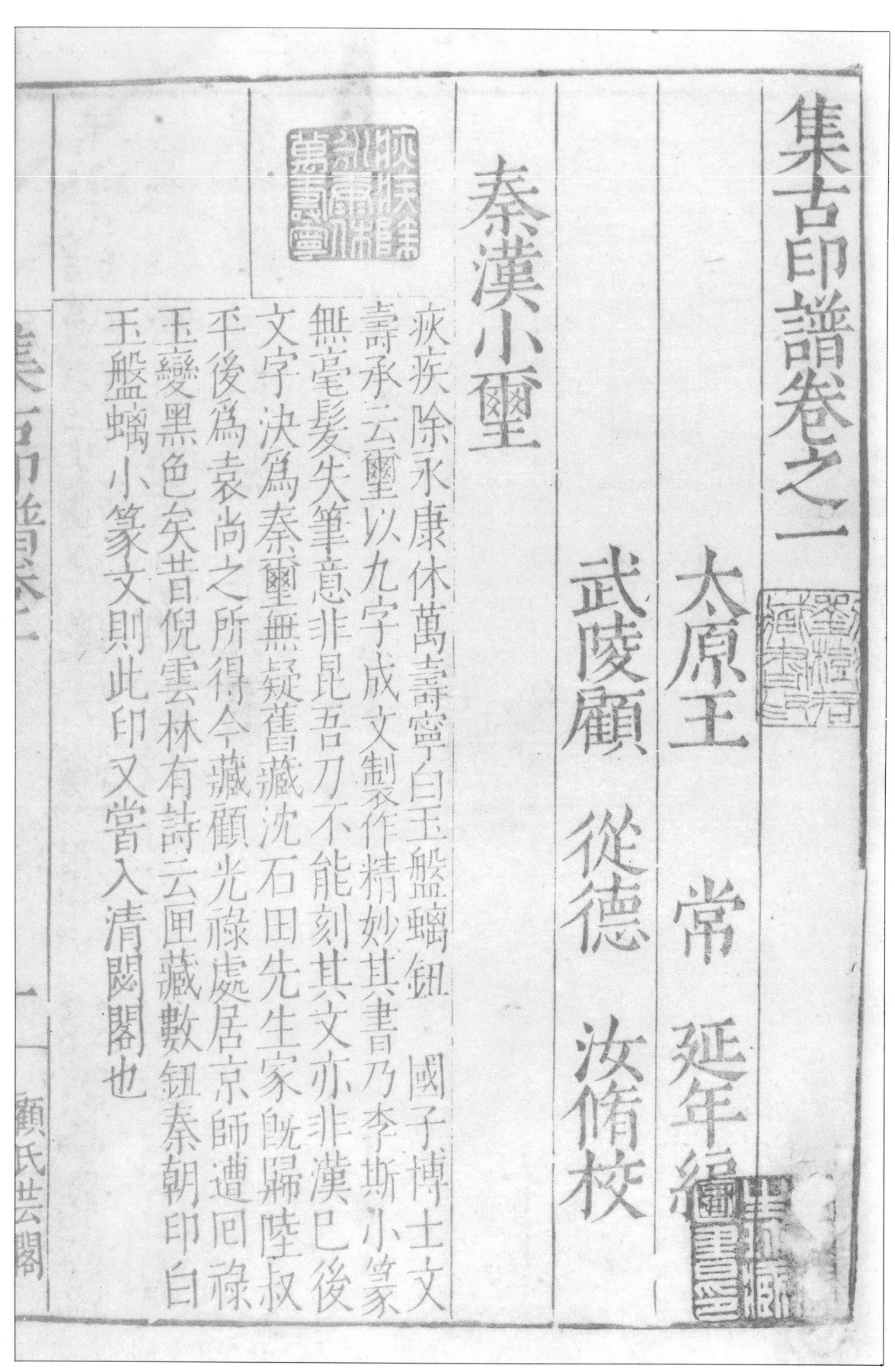

集古印譜卷之一

太原王　常　延年編
武陵顧從德　汝脩校

秦漢小璽

狄狄除永康休萬壽寧白玉盤螭鈕壽承云璽以九字成文製作精妙其書乃李斯小篆無毫髮失筆意非昆吾刀不能刻其文亦非漢巳後文字決為秦璽無疑舊藏沈石田先生家既歸陸叔平後為袁尚之所得今藏顧光祿處居京師遭囘祿玉變黑色矣昔倪雲林有詩云匣藏數鈕秦朝印白玉盤螭小篆文則此印又嘗入清閟閣也

Pl. 58, (No. 42). Gu Congde (b. ca. 1520), compiler, **Jigu yinpu**.
Ming dynasty, dated 1575. Leaf from a woodblock printed book of seal impressions. Guanhai Lou Collection

popular during the late Northern Song period as part of the literati interest in epigraphy and archaeology. The *Xiaotang jigulu* by the Northern Song scholar Wang Qiu, for example, recorded thirty-seven ancient seals; its main purpose, however, was more antiquarian than artistic. But most other Song *yinpu* are either lost or not reliable.[107]

It was during the Ming dynasty that *yinpu* began to be produced in great quantity. Based in part on earlier *yinpu*, Gu Congde's *Jigu yinpu* of 1575 recorded about 160 jade seals and more than 1,600 bronze seals (No. 42, Pl. 58).[108] *Yinpu* devoted to a single seal engraver or a group of seal engravers also began to be produced. The main purpose of these *yinpu* was for emulation and appreciation. Zhu Jian's (active 1572-1620) *Yinjing*, in six *juan* (chapters/volumes), was compiled in 1611 to illustrate the principles of composition of seal legends and construction of characters.[109] A large number of Ming *yinpu*, however, lost the subtle quality of the original seals as a result of imprecise reproduction. Furthermore, like late Ming books in general, they also suffered from mass production out of commercial interest.

First published in 1647 under the title of *Yincun*, Hu Yuecong's (1584-1674) *Yincun chuji*, dated to 1661 and now in the collection of Wang Fang-yu, is an important example of late Ming and early Qing *yinpu* (No. 43, Color pl. 3). One of the most important publishers of his time, Hu Yuecong, was himself an accomplished seal engraver.[110] *Laigutang yinpu* (preface dated 1667) was compiled by the children of the seventeenth century art patron Zhou Lianggong. It recorded about seven hundred seals from the collection of Zhou Lianggong; all the impressions were reproduced with extreme care in order to maintain fidelity to the seals themselves.[111]

During the later part of the Qing dynasty, as part of the intellectual pursuits of the Evidential Research (*Kaozhengxue*) and Bronze-and-Stone Studies (*Jinshixue*) movements, the production of *yinpu* became more faithful to the original seals. The increasingly large number of *yinpu* during the eighteenth and nineteenth centuries is an indication of the high regard that seal engraving had in the cultural life of the Chinese educated elite (No. 44, Pl. 60; No. 45, Pl. 57; No. 46, Pl. 59; No. 47, Color pls. 6A-C; No. 50, Pl. 7). Furthermore, the large proportion of elegant literary phrases (about 80 percent), as opposed to personal names, on the more than four thousand Ming and Qing seals collected and recorded by Wang Qishu (1728-1800) in his highly popular *Feihongtang yinpu* (preface dated 1745) indicates that seal engraving was a unique and independent art form (No. 44, Pl. 60). Sometimes a whole literary composition such as the celebrated "Returning Home" (*Guiqulaici*) by Tao Qian (365-427) would be transcribed in the form of a large number of seals engraved in a variety of compositional schemes, as seen in *Xiaoshi shanfang yinpu*, compiled by Gu Xiang and Gu Hao and published in 1828 (No. 46, Pl. 59).

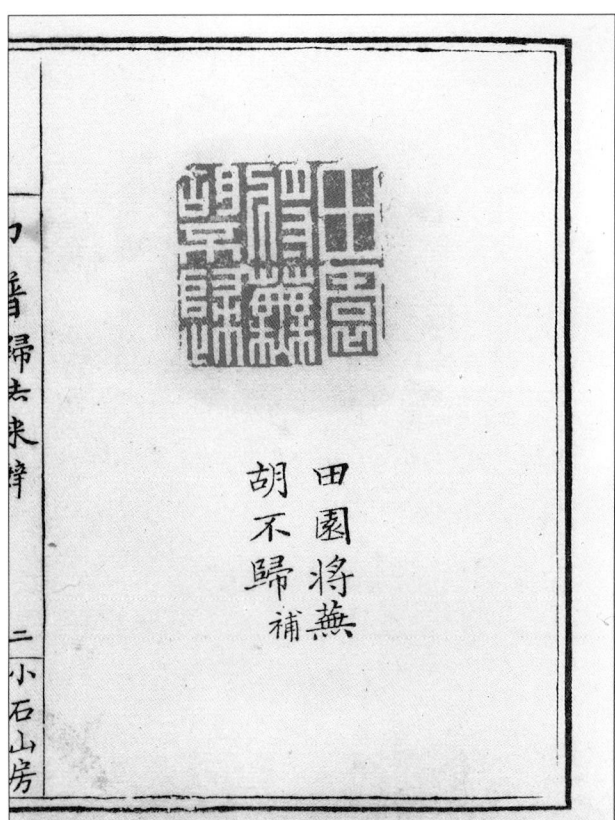

Pl. 59, (No. 46). Gu Xiang and Gu Hao (active early 19th c.), compilers, **Xiaoshi shanfang yinpu**. Qing dynasty, dated 1831. Leaf from a woodblock printed book of seal impressions. Gest Oriental Library and East Asian Collections, Princeton University, New Jersey

In many ways, the best *yinpu*, in which the impressions and the reproductions (rubbings) are done by hand, can be considered a category of artists' books because of their artistry and limited number of copies. They are works of art in themselves, commanding high prices among the connoisseurs. One example is the *Wu Rangzhi yinpu*, now in the collection of Dr. Sesin Jong (No. 47, Color pls. 6A-C).[112]

Seal Impressions as Part of Calligraphy or Painting

The use of an artist's seal on a piece of calligraphy or painting probably began during the Northern Song dynasty, particularly within the circles of such literati as Mi Fu, Su Shi, and Ouyang Xiu. Although the joining of a literary text and a painting can be traced as far back as the Six Dynasties period, it was during the Yuan dynasty, with the rise of a more calligraphic and expressive style of painting, that actual calligraphy began to appear on the pictorial surface as an integral part of the composition. Starting in the Yuan dynasty, personal seals of artists began to be used increasingly on calligraphy or painting. Personal seals served pri-

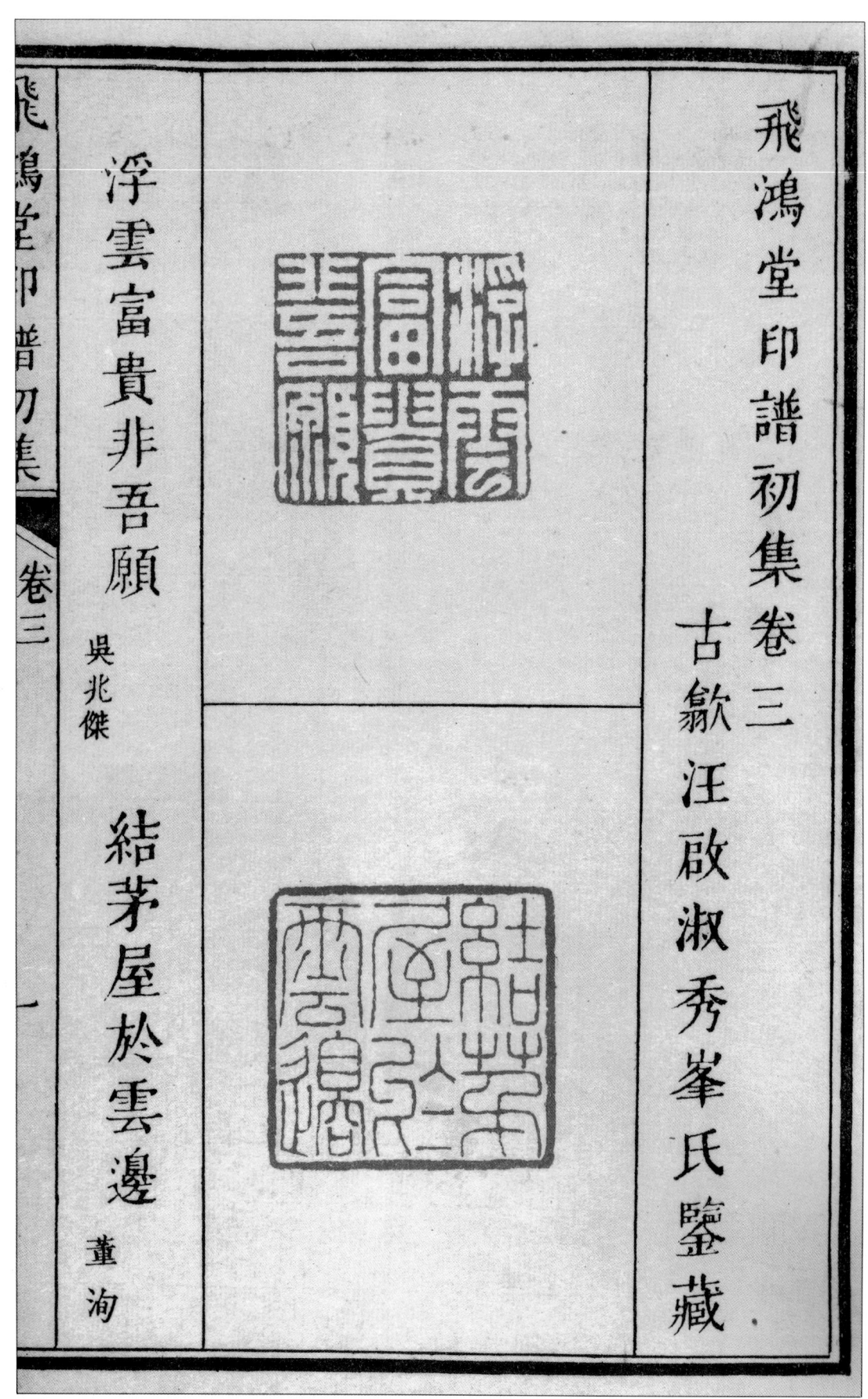

Pl. 60, (No. 44). Wang Qishu (1728-1800), compiler, **Feihong tang yinpu**. Qing dynasty, dated 1776. Leaf from a woodblock printed book of seal impressions.
Gest Oriental Library and East Asian Collections, Princeton University, New Jersey

marily to indicate authorship—or ownership, in the case of a collector.

In addition to the seal with the name of the artist, a more personal seal, called *xianzhang*, or leisure seal, began to be used more frequently, adding another dimension to the expressive content of the work.[113] Examples of *xianzhang* include Numbers 29 (Pl. 61), 37, 35, and 40A. It is the use of such seals that enriches the compositional and semantic potential of a painting. For instance, a type of seal, called *yajiaozhang*, or balancing-corner seal, is often placed in the lower right or lower left corner to serve as a balance to the colophon in the upper left or right corner. One example is the seal *Xueran sanren* (A Carefree Person Who Is Like the Glistening Plumage of Birds) that follows the first line of the dedication on the calligraphy couplet by Xu Sangeng (No. 61, Color pl. 9). Another type of compositional seal is called *qishouzhang* or *yinshouzhang* (colophon-head seal) which is placed in the upper right-hand corner of a colophon. Both types are clearly compositional devices. They have often been employed by such modern masters as Qi Baishi and Pan Tianshou (1897-1971). As Pan Tianshou himself pointed out, in traditional Chinese painting, "seals and inscriptions are an integral part of the content of a painting; their relations are inseparable like blood and flesh and cannot be placed without any preconception." He also maintained that even the size of the seal and the spacing of the legend must be considered part of the composition. Furthermore, the vermilion impressions of the seals must be carefully balanced with the ink tonalities of the pictorial image and the inscription of a painting.[114] This balance is achieved, for instance, in the fan painting *Apricot*, by Wu Xizai (No. 58, Color pl. 7).

Many examples of the integration of seals with the pictorial image and inscription of a painting can be cited. For instance, the late Ming artist Zhu Da, also called Badashanren (1626-1705), whose compositions exerted a strong influence on many later artists, placed a seal in the shape of a mountain on his pair of small album leaves *Flower and Calligraphy*, dated 1690, now in the collection of Wang Fang-yu and Sum Wai Wang (Pl. 62; Fig. 5). As Richard Barnhart has observed, the seal adds an important and integral dimension to the artistic import of this painting:

> What looks like the impress of open lips has nothing to do with lips, but is a picture of a white mountain enclosed in red. White is the color of mourning, and red is *zhu*, which is Bada's [Zhu Da's] name and the name of the Ming imperial family. But seals are always red, so [why] is a red seal containing a white mountain significant? Spring was the season in which the last Ming emperor died; this picture was painted in spring; a strange seal that could be read as a lament for the former Ming dynasty is dramatically placed beneath the signature of Bada Shanren.[115]

Pl. 61, (No. 29). **Double-Sided Seal in the Shape of an Ancient Coin**. Probably Qing dynasty (1644-1912). Soapstone. Dr. Paul Singer

As a matter of fact, the seals on Badashanren's paintings constitute one of the major keys to the meaning of his art.

Collector's Seals

The eighteenth-century connoisseur Lu Shihua, in his *Shuhuashuoling* of 1776, gave the following advice on using collectors' seals:

> Collectors' seals should not be stamped arbitrarily on a painting or autograph, for these seals have their fixed places. In some cases you should use a large seal, in others a smaller one; sometimes seals with red legends, at others seals with white legends. And if there should be no suitable place left on a scroll, then you had better leave it without your seals.[116]

Apart from the incorrect and excessive placement of seals, the abuse of collectors' seals also includes the use of genuine seals by forgers on fakes. As Lu Shihua pointed out: "Collectors' seals of connoisseurs of former times and seals bearing the appellations of famous people can often still be found. Forgers will borrow those seals and impress them on seams of their fakes, which they have moreover mounted in a most luxurious manner, 'with title-labels written in gold and jade roller knobs.'"[117] Many examples of forged artists' seals and collectors' seals can be cited. For instance, Sherman Lee and Wai-kam Ho have published a list of paintings spuriously purported to be from the collection of Liang

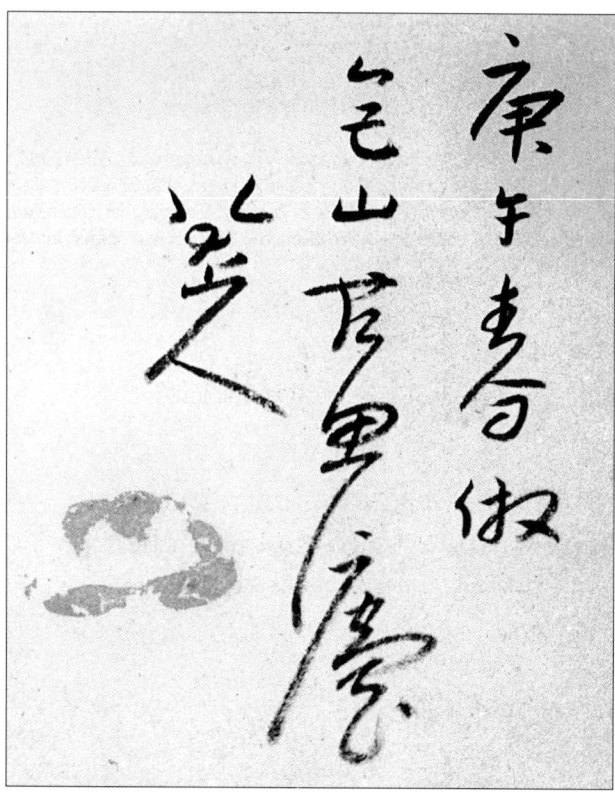

Pl. 62 (Fig. 5). Bada Shanren (1626-1705), **Flower and Calligraphy**. Dated 1690. Album leaf, ink and light colors on paper. Wang Fang-yu and Sum Wai Wang

Meihua'an as Wu Zhen's (1280-1354). However, he mistakenly inferred that Wu Zhen was the collector; stylistic examination reveals that the painting is by Wu Zhen himself.[122]

In some cases, the same legend may actually appear on seals that belong to different persons. For example, two seals that contain the legend *Chang* have been discovered; one belongs to Jia Sidao of the Southern Song dynasty, the other to the seventeenth-century collector Geng Jiazuo.[123] In this case, the quality of the work of art should obviously be the most important consideration.

By studying the seals of collectors, we are aided in establishing the history of taste and patronage as an important aspect of art history, an aspect explored by the studies on Liang Qingbiao by Sherman Lee and Wai-kam Ho, and on Anhui merchants as art patrons by the present author.[124] As Wang Chi-ch'ien and Kathleen Yang point out: "While careful connoisseurship, objective scholarship, and familiarity with the brushwork and calligraphic stroke of an individual artist are major elements in deciding the authenticity of a Chinese painting, seals themselves can often play a significant role in this process."[125] Through methodical study and comparison of impressions that appear on known, authenticated paintings, a reference collection of reliable seal impressions can be obtained. Although the process has begun, more needs to be done.[126]

Qingbiao (1620-1691), the great connoisseur and collector of the seventeenth century.[118]

It should be noted that sometimes a genuine painting may also bear forged seals of collectors, as demonstrated by Na Zhiliang in reference to seals allegedly belonging to Xiang Yuanbian (1525-1590), the great Ming-dynasty collector, on a number of paintings in the National Palace Museum, Taipei.[119] Other examples of forged collectors' seals have been published by Luo Fuyi.[120] Although the presence of genuine seals of a famous collector on a work of art may sometimes help the connoisseur in the dating, authentication, and history of the work of art, they must be viewed with extreme care and reservation. It is also possible that a genuine collector's seal may be found on a misattributed work of art. In this case, the date of the genuine seal can be used as a *terminus ad quem* for a work of art. For example, all paintings that bear the half-seal *Siyin* must be dated no later than 1384, because that particular seal ceased to be used by the Ming court office after that year.[121]

The originator of a seal on a painting may be misidentified as a collector when he is actually the creator of that painting. A good example is the hanging scroll *Autumn Mountains* (*Qiushantu*), in the National Palace Museum, which had long been attributed to Juran (active ca. 960-80) by such connoisseurs as Dong Qichang, who correctly regarded the seal impression

Notes

1. Wu Qi (ca. 1647), as cited in *LY*, 2: 611.

2. Quoted in Gaur, 185.

3. The artist may allow the seal to substitute for his signature. When his seal is absent, it is often an indication that the work is incomplete or that the artist was not pleased with it.

4. Fry, 3.

5. A significant difference between a rubbing and a seal impression is that the latter creates an image in reverse as does printing. According to Tsuen-hsuin Tsien, "Before printing was used in China, many techniques for making reproductions existed. At first, of course, texts were copied by hand, but later mechanical devices were devised. These included seals for stamping on clay and, in due course, on silk and paper; the casting and engraving of inscriptions on metal and stone, the taking of inked impressions from stone inscriptions and, finally, using stencils to duplicate designs on textiles and paper. All these processes paved the way for the use of woodblock printing and later printing from movable type" (Tsien [1985], 133).

6. See Li Guojun, 1026-92.

7. Ehrenwerth; Veit; Wagner (1987).

8. Van Gulik (1958a), 417-57. More recently, in the spring of 1992 the Yale University Art Gallery held an exhibition entitled, "The World Within a Square: The Art of Chinese Seal Carving." It was curated by Qianshen Bai, a seal carver and graduate student, and was a significant step in the right direction. Unfortunately, it was not accompanied by a catalogue.

9. Wilhelm, 328.
10. Keightley, 198.
11. Quoted by Zhang Huaiguan, in *LS*, 158-160; translation amended from Huot.
12. Quoted in Li Shu-hua, 71-72.
13. Barnhart (1964).
14. Yang Xiong, in *ZMZ*, 1: 116.
15. Wang Fang-yu (1958), v.
16. Wang Fang-yu (1958), vii.
17. *SZ*, 1: 44-45, pls. 131-134.
18. Trans. and quoted in Driscoll and Toda, 26.
19. Ledderose (1972), 5.
20. *SZ*, vol. 1, pls. 138-139.
21. For a discussion of these ideas, see Cahill (1976).
22. Fong (1976), 93.
23. Quoted in Elman, 190-91.
24. Chen Jieqi's book on seals, *Shizhong shanfang yinju*, was published 1872 and again in 1904 (No. 50, Pl. 7). *Fengni kaolue* of 1904 by Wu Shifen and Chen Jieqi reproduces clay sealings (No. 51, Pls. 8, 9). Yang Shoujing's *Guquansou* reproduces rubbings of coins (No. 3, Pl. 6).
25. Ledderose (1970).
26. Shen C. Y. Fu et al. (1977), 55.
27. Barnhart (1972), 233.
28. Barnhart (1972), 233.
29. Addis et al., 51.
30. *LS*, 129; trans. in Sun Ta-yü, 202.
31. Wang Fang-yu (1988), 44.
32. National Palace Museum, 48-53.
33. *ZMQ*, 43: 6.
34. Luo Fuyi and Wang Rencong, 2-3.
35. Tsien (1985), 139-40.
36. *ZMQ*, vol. 43, pls. 24.17, 30; vol. 49, pls. 1-25, 90-107.
37. *ZMQ*, vol. 43, pls. 33-34; vol. 49, pls. 26-36, 111-124.
38. See also Ecke, no. 5A.
39. Quoted in *LY*, 1: 210.
40. Wang Zhongshu, figs. 206-210.
41. *ZMQ*, vol. 43, pls. 65, 67, 68; *SZ*, vol. 2, pls. 52, 55.
42. *SZ*, vol. 1, pls. 104-105.
43. Fong (1980), 332; for a compendium on *niaochongshu* see Hou Fuchang.
44. *ZMQ*, vol. 43, pls. 42-43, 46-48, 51-53; vol. 49, pls. 37-72, 125-174.
45. Cheng Te-k'un, 137-167.
46. Luo Suizu, 92-96.
47. *LY*, 1: 11-32.
48. Sha Menghai, 97; for Wu Yan's 1305 colophon to a handscroll *Zhang Hao-hao shi* by Du Mu, now in the Palace Museum, Beijing, and two of his seals, see Shen C. Y. Fu et al. (1977), fig. 24.
49. Shen C. Y. Fu et al., 190-91.
50. Luo Fuyi and Wang Rencong, 32.
51. According to Liu Yunhe, a stone seal was excavated from a Warring States tomb at Shanbiaozhen and about 50 stone seals were found in Western Han tombs at Changsha. Furthermore, a tomb dated 445 from Fuzhou yielded evidence that Shoushan stone was already quarried by the fifth century, if not earlier. Therefore, Wang Mian could not have been the first to use soapstone for seals. See Liu Yunhe, "Chuangshi kezhi shiyin chutan (On the origins of stone seal engraving)," *SP*, no. 46 (June 1982), p. 13.
52. For an example, see Neill et al., 106-8.
53. Watt, in Li and Watt, 11.
54. Qian and Ye, 82-83.
55. Quoted in Kuo (1991), 26.
56. For a biography of Huang Yi, see *CTS*, 14: 161-63.
57. For a biography of Chen Hongshou, see *CTS*, 16: 207-17.
58. For a biography of Zhao Zhishen see *CTS*, 17: 185-90.
59. For a biography of Qian Song, see *CTS*, 18: 181-87.
60. *LY*, 2: 705-6.
61. Trans. in Ecke, no. 96.
62. Ma Guoquan.
63. For a biography of Zhao Zhiqian, see *CTS*, vols. 26-27.
64. Quoted and trans. in Bennett, 210.
65. Fong, unpublished paper (1989), 7.
66. Billeter, 263.
67. Yu Jianhua, 30-31.
68. Wang and Li, 44, 50.
69. *CTS*, vol. 37.
70. Fong, unpublished paper (1989).
71. Beijing tushuguan, 1: 24.
72. Quoted in Fu Baoshi, 129-30.
73. Quoted in Fu Baoshi, 130.
74. Yang Guangtai, 28.
75. For a recent study, see Kuo (1989b).
76. *LY*, 1: 462-81.
77. Ellsworth, 210.
78. *CTS*, 40: 100-101, 194-96.
79. Shen C. Y. Fu (1987), 77.
80. For a biography of Zhao Shigang, see *CTS*, 39: 177-78.
81. Ellsworth, 192.
82. For a biography of Zhao Shi, see *CTS*, 40: 187-88.
83. Li Guojun, 1003.
84. For a biography of Deng Sanmu, see *CTS*, 40: 198-99.
85. Quoted in *SP*, no. 85 (June 1988): 70.
86. Quoted in *LY*, 2: 604.
87. Ye Erkuan, 136-37; translation amended from Ye Qiuyuan.
88. Quoted in *LY*, 2: 616.

89. Edwards (1987), 122.

90. Quoted in *LY*, 2: 611-12.

91. Chen Zizhuang, 137.

92. Shen Fu, *Fusheng liuji*, trans. in Lin Yutang, 995.

93. Zheng Xie, 176; translation amended from Song Shouquan, 168.

94. The passage was translated by Lin Yutang as "[to] provide for the real in the unreal and for the unreal real in the real" (Lin Yutang, 995).

95. Trans. in Waley (1958), 155.

96. Trans. in Coleman, 120-21.

97. Powers, 162-63.

98. Hay (1983), 74-104.

99. Dondis, 104-27.

100. Li Shuhua, 73-84.

101. Watt, in Li and Watt, 11.

102. *LY*, 2: 969; translation amended from Lai, 5-6.

103. For stimulating discussions on stones in Chinese art and culture, see Hay (1986); for a post-modernist interpretation see Jing Wang (1992).

104. Mowry, in Li and Watt, 172-73.

105. Wang Beiyue (1991), 36-38; the following descriptions of methods of using the knife in seal engraving are indebted to Chiang Yee (1973), chap. 5.

106. Van Gulik (1958a), 87-90.

107. Xiao Gaohong.

108. Han Tianheng (1990) suggests that the 1575 edition, also called *Yinsou*, is a woodcut version of an earlier (1572), hand-impressed edition, of which a copy is in the Xie collection in Shanghai.

109. *LY*, 1: 160-67.

110. *CTS*, 5: 122-49, 172-74.

111. *CTS*, 8: 143-50.

112. For a detailed discussion of seal books, see Yokota Minoru.

113. For *xianzhang*, see Zhu Xuchu; also see Huangshi laoren.

114. Pan Tianshou, 33, 51-52.

115. Barnhart, in Wang and Barnhart, 110-11.

116. Trans. in van Gulik (1958b), 51-52.

117. Trans. in van Gulik (1958b), 27-28.

118. Lee and Ho, 146-51.

119. Na Zhiliang (1956).

120. Luo Fuyi (1974).

121. Suzuki, 34-39; Zhuang Shen, 1-46.

122. Wang Shijie, pl. 45.

123. Wang Chi-ch'ien and Yang (1988).

124. Lee and Ho (1980); Kuo (1989a).

125. Wang Chi-ch'ien and Yang (1988), 151.

126. Studies include Contag and Wang; *Zhongguo shuhuajia yinjian kuanshi*; Edwards (1963); Wang Chi-ch'ien (1957); Winter and Ellentuck.

COLOR PLATES

Color pl. 1, (No. 14). **Bronze Seal with Tortoise Knob**. Han dynasty (206 B.C.-A.D. 220). Anonymous

Color pl. 2, (No 16). **Official Seal with Knob in the Shape of a Tortoise**. Six Dynasties Period (265-589). Gilt bronze. Dr. Paul Singer

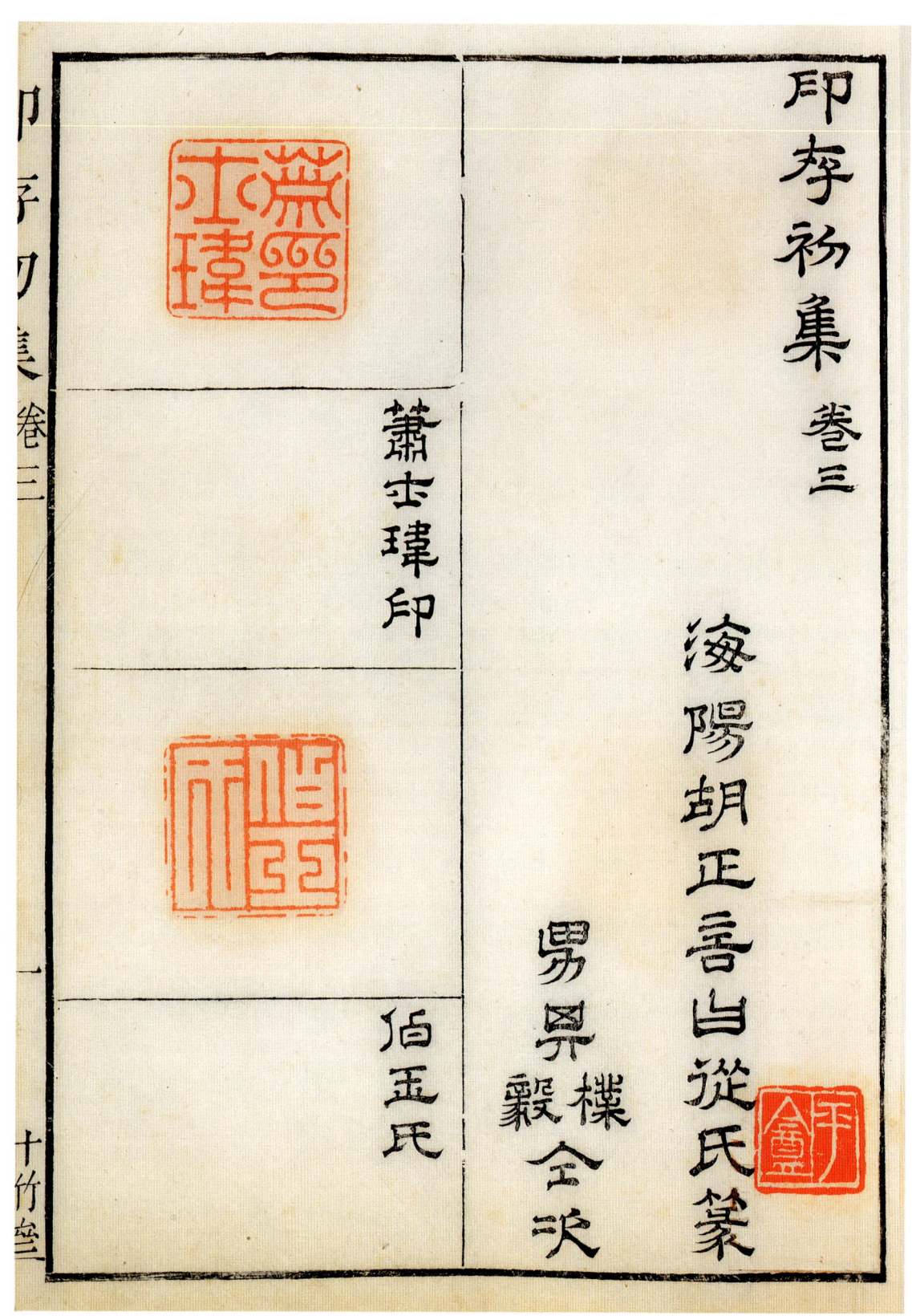

Color pl. 3, (No. 43). Hu Zhengyen (mid-17th c.), compiler, **Yincun chuji**. Qing dynasty, dated 1661. Leaf from a woodblock printed book of seal impressions. Wang Fang-yu and Sum Wai Wang

Color pl. 4, (No. 28). Huang Wenhan (active late 19th c.), **Double-Sided Seal**. Qing dynasty, dated 1881. Ivory. Dr. Paul Singer

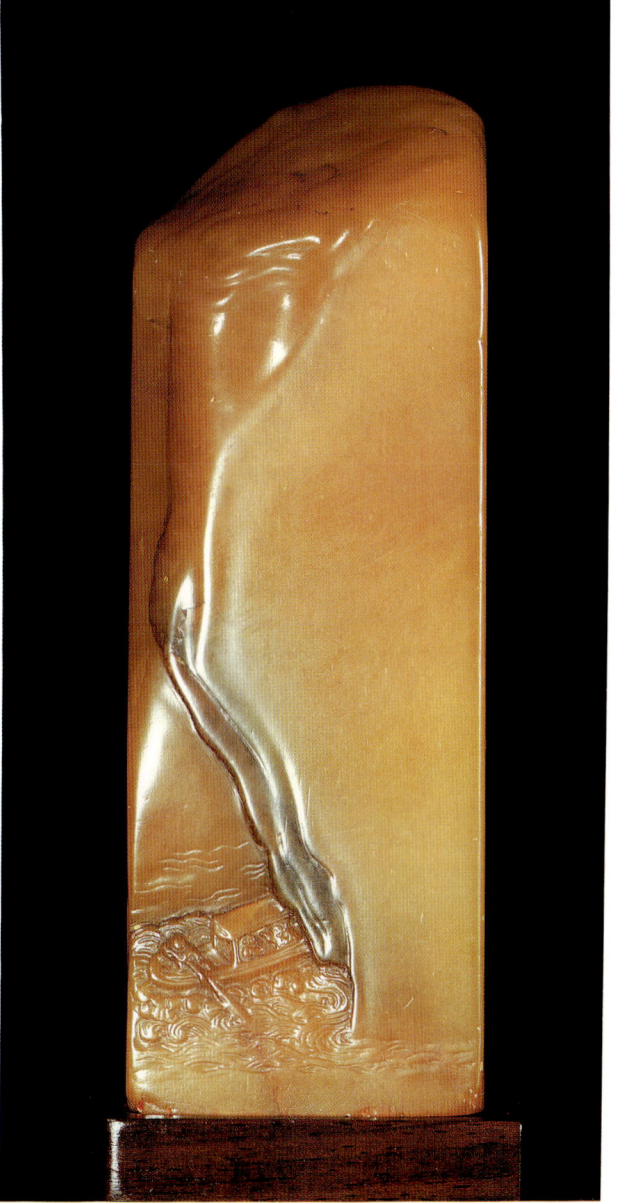

Color pl. 5 (No. 26). Qian Song (1807-1860), **Seal**. Qing dynasty. Shoushan stone, *tianhuang* type. On loan to The Brooklyn Museum from The Guennol Collection

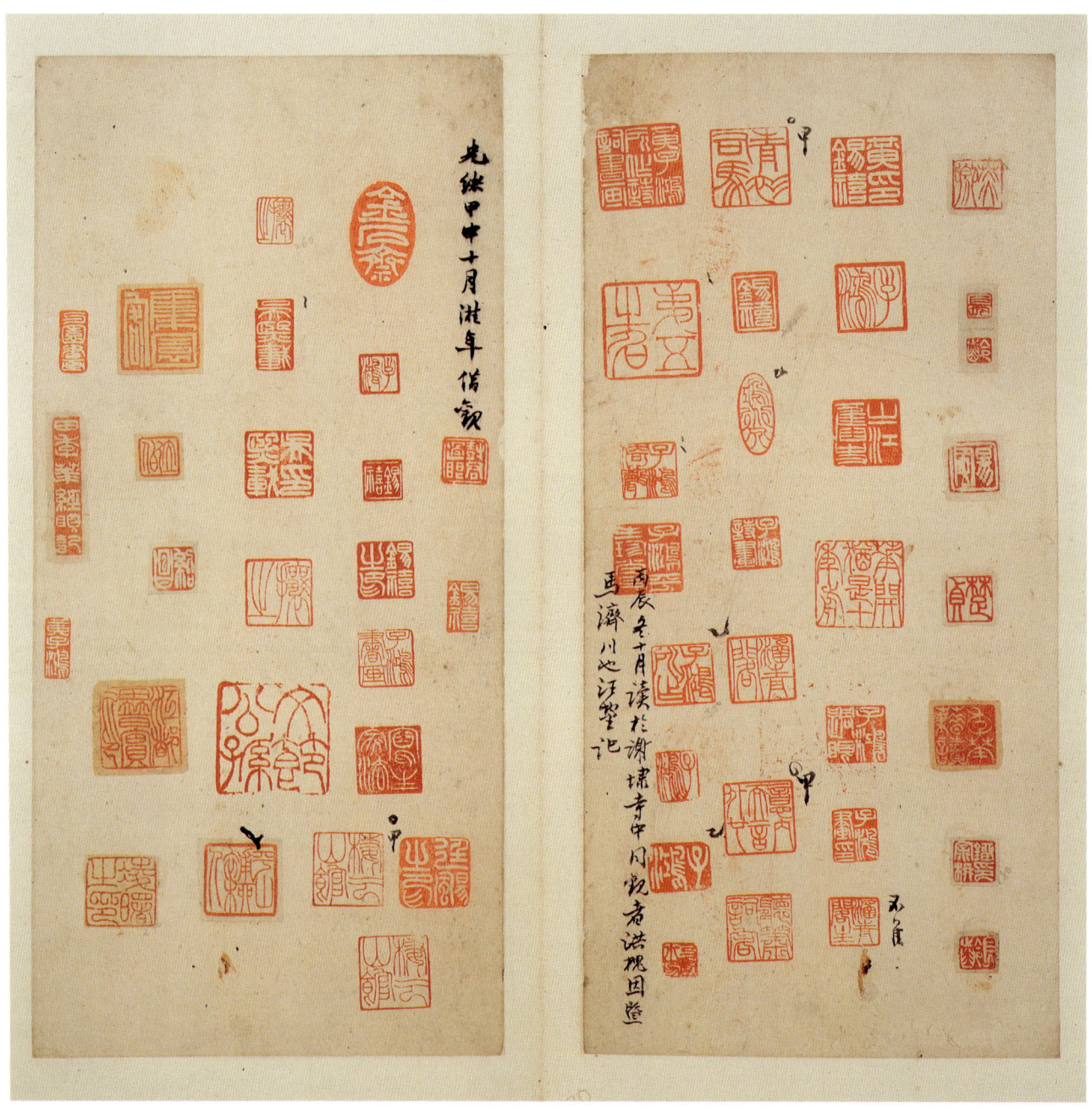

A

Color pl. 6A-C, (No. 47). Wu Xizai (1799-1870), **Wu Rangzhi yinpu**.
Qing dynasty, 19th c. Leaves from a book of seal impressions.
Dr. Sesin Jong

B

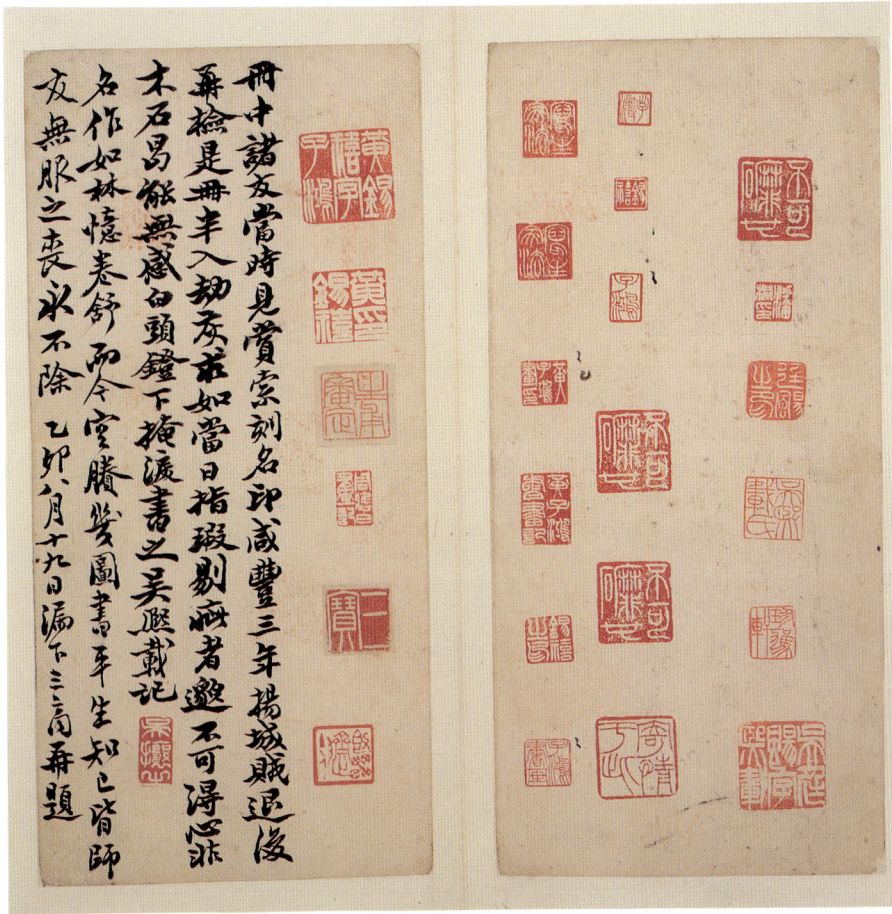

册中諸友當時見賞家刻名印咸豐三年楊城賊退後
余檢是冊半入刧灰並如當日指瑕剔疵者邈不可得心非
木石曷能無感白頭鐙下掩淚書之吳熙載記
名作如林憶卷舒而今室膡縈圖書平生知己皆師
友無服之喪永不除 乙卯八月十九日漏下三鼓再題

C

Color pl. 7, (No. 58). Wu Xizai (1799-1870), **Apricot**. Fan painting.
The Metropolitan Museum of Art, New York; Gift of Robert Hatfield Ellsworth
in memory of La Ferne Hatfield Ellsworth, 1986

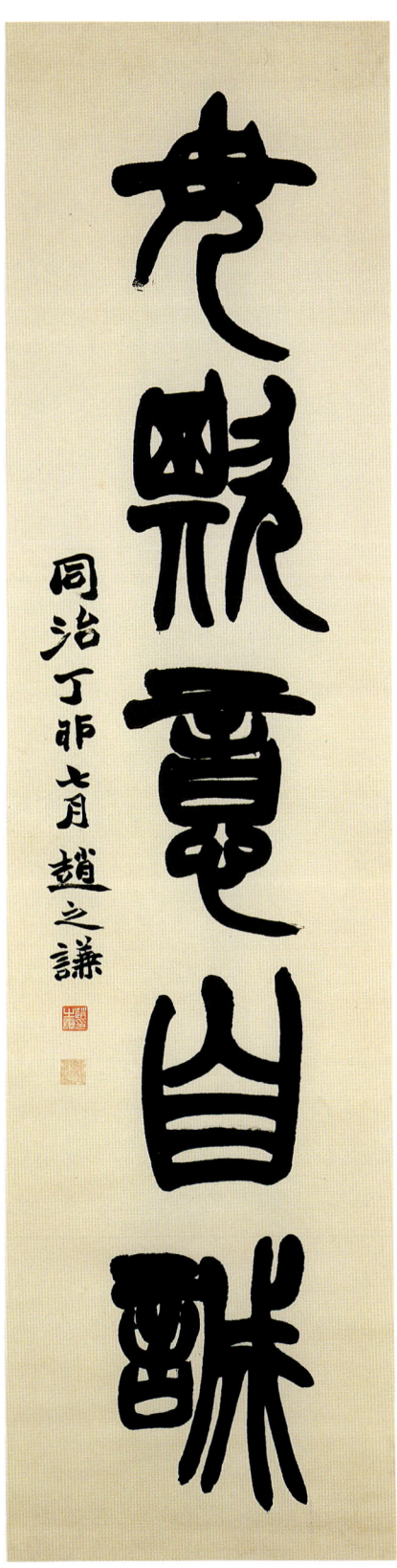
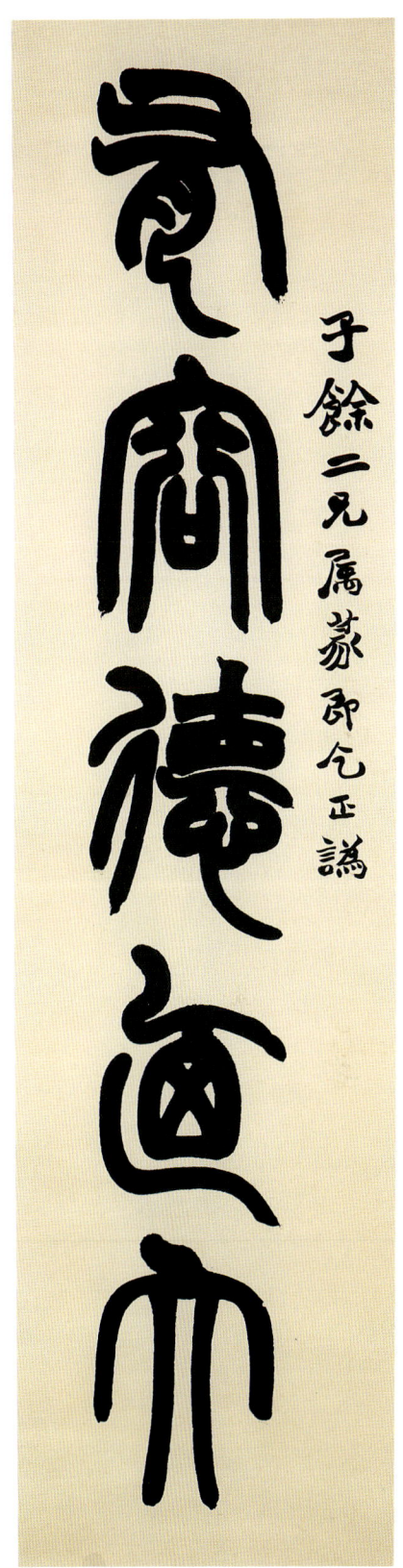

Color pl. 8, (No. 60). Zhao Zhiqian (1829-1884), **Calligraphy in Seal Script**. Qing dynasty, dated 1867. Pair of hanging scrolls.
F. Randall and Judith G. Smith

Color pl. 9, (No. 61). Xu Sangeng (1826-1890),
Meet the Plum and Moon by Chance.
Qing dynasty, dated 1887. Pair of hanging scrolls.
Robert Hatfield Ellsworth

CATALOGUE OF THE EXHIBITION

SOURCES OF THE ART OF SEAL ENGRAVING

1. (Pl. 1)
Rubbing of Inscriptions from the Ten Stone Drums (8-3rd c. B.C.)
Ming dynasty (1368-1644)
Handscroll, ink on paper, 17 3/4 x 22 5/8 in.
(45.1 x 57.5 cm)
The Metropolitan Museum of Art, New York; Promised Gift of Wan-go H. C. and Virginia Weng, 1989
Published: Ecke, no. 4

The poem reproduced here reads:

> Our chariots are well-worked through and through;
> Our horses are thoroughly matched.
> Our chariots are perfectly in order;
> Our horses are thoroughly robust.
>
> The noblemen are about to go hunting,
> They are about to go hunting and about to roam.
> The hinds and stags are nimble;
> The noblemen are in search of them.
>
> Well-aligned are the horn bows.
> With bow and string we await [our prey].
> We drive out the bulls,
> Their approach resounds with the clatter of hoofs.
> They go scampering and moving on.
> Now we drive, now we stop.
>
> The hinds and stags are frenzied;
> Their advance is ever so wild.
> We drive out the bucks;
> Their advance is marked by the thud of hoofs.
> We shoot the full-grown ones. . . .
>   (Trans. Mattos, 165-166)

2. (Pl. 10)
Coin
Warring States Period (475-221 B.C.)
Bronze, 1 3/4 x 1 1/2 in. (4.5 x 3.8 cm)
Inscribed: *Qiu bei* (coin from the city of Qiu)
Yale University Art Gallery, New Haven; Gift of Professor and Mrs. Hans H. Frankel

Qiu may refer to any of a number of cities from the state of Wei (Zheng Jiaxiang, 93-97).

3. (Pl. 6)
Yang Shoujing (1839-1914), compiler
Guquansou
Woodblock printed book, 10 3/8 x 5 7/8 x 7/16 in.
(26.4 x 14.9 x 1.2 cm)
Gest Oriental Library and East Asian Collections, Princeton University, New Jersey

On one side of each of the coins reproduced in Plate 6 there is a two-character inscription, *An yang*, which indicates that these coins were made in the city of Anyi (in modern Shanxi province) in the state of Wei during the Warring States period (see Zheng Jiaxiang, pp. 94-95). Probably because of their unassuming simplicity, inscriptions on ancient coins have been an important source for seal engravers in search of antique flavors.

Yang Shoujing was an accomplished calligrapher and a scholar of ancient geography, books, and coins.

4. (Pls. 11, 16)
Molded Roof Tile Terminal
Qin or Han dynasty (3rd century B.C.)
Pottery, length: 19 9/16 in. (50.3 cm),
diam.: 6 5/8 in. (17 cm)
Inscribed: *Changle weiyang* (Happy forever, without end, or Long joy at Wei-yang Palace)
Field Museum of Natural History, Chicago; nos. 118944A, B
Published: Tsien (1962), pl. X

The top of the tile has been modified in more recent times to be used as a grinding stone for ink sticks.

SEALS

5. (Pl. 15B)
Silver Seal
Warring States Period (475-221 B.C.)
Height: 1 3/16 in. (3 cm)
Intaglio legend (indecipherable)
Dr. Paul Singer

The knob of the seal is in the shape of a pillar.

6. (Pl. 15A)
Lacquer Seal
Warring States Period (475-221 B.C.)
Height: 5/8 in. (1.6 cm)
Intaglio legend: *Zhou Rong*
Dr. Paul Singer

7. (Pl. 19A)
Jade Seal
Han dynasty (206 B.C.-A.D. 220)
Height: 11/16 in. (1.7 cm)
Intaglio square legend: *Wu Ling*
Dr. Paul Singer

8. (Pl. 19B)
Jade Seal
Han dynasty (206 B.C.-A.D. 220)
Height: 11/16 in. (1.8 cm)
Intaglio square legend: *Sima wengzhi*
Dr. Paul Singer

9. (Pl. 19C)
Jade Seal
Han dynasty (206 B.C.-A.D. 220)
Height: 3/8 in. (1 cm)
Intaglio rectangular legend: *Yin Zhang*
Dr. Paul Singer

10. (Pl. 19D)
Pictorial Seal
Han dynasty (206 B.C.-A.D. 220)
Jade, 9/16 x 7/16 x 3/8 in. (1.5 x 1.2 x 1 cm)
Dr. Paul Singer

The seal has an intaglio legend depicting a deer.

11. (Pl. 18)
Pictorial Seal
Han dynasty (206 B.C.-A.D. 220)
Bronze, diam.: 13/16 in. (2 cm)
Dr. Paul Singer

The seal has an intaglio legend depicting a crane or swan; its knob is in the shape of a snake.

12. (Pl. 20)
Clay Seal Impression
Han dynasty (206 B.C.-A.D. 220)
Length: 15/16 in. (2.4 cm)
Intaglio legend: *Xinye cheng yin* (Seal of the magistrate at Xinye)
Field Museum of Natural History, Chicago; no. 117030
Published: Tsien (1962), pl. VIII.D

13. (Pl. 17)
Three Clay Impressions of Pictorial Seals
Seals from Han dynasty (206 B.C.-A.D. 220),
    modern impressions
A. Diam., 14/16 in. (2.2 cm)
B. 11/16 x 7/16 in. (1.8 x 1.2 cm)
C. 7/16 x 7/16 in. (1.2 x 1.2 cm)
Private collection

14. (Color pl. 1)
Bronze Seal with Tortoise Knob
Han dynasty (206 B.C.-A.D. 220)
Height: 1/2 in. (1.3 cm)
Intaglio legend: *Li Tian siyin* (Private seal of Li Tian)
Anonymous

15. (Pl. 21)
Official Seal with Figure of Reclining Camel as Knob
Wei dynasty (Three Kingdoms Period, [221-65])
Bronze, height: 15/16 in. (2.4 cm)
Intaglio legend: *Wei shuai shan di baizhang* (Official of the Di tribe under the Wei dynasty)
Field Museum of Natural History, Chicago; no. 117044

For a similar seal in the Palace Museum, see Luo Fuyi (1982a), 70, no. 387.

16. (Color pl. 2)
Official Seal with Knob in the Shape of a Tortoise
Six Dynasties Period (265-589)
Gilt bronze, height: 2 1/16 in. (5.2 cm)
Intaglio Square legend: *Fubo jiangjun zhang*
Dr. Paul Singer

For a similar seal, see Luo Fuyi (1981a), 74. Such seals belong to a type of military official seal that was usually engraved in haste, resulting in the crudeness seen here. Later seal engravers, however, have tried to emulate them in order to achieve the effect of archaism.

17. (Pl. 22)
Official Seal
Song dynasty, dated 1055
Bronze, 1 9/16 x 1 9/16 x 1 in. (4 x 4 x 2.5 cm)
Relief legend: *Jian'nan Dongchuan jiedushi yin*
            (Seal of the Commander at Jian'nan and Dongchuan regions)
Field Museum of Natural History, Chicago; no. 117059

18. (Pl. 23)
Official Seal
Yuan dynasty, dated 1308
Bronze, 1 5/8 x 1 5/8 x 15/16 in. (4.2 x 4.2 x 2.4 cm)
Relief legend: *Zhenhaijun jiedushi zhiyin* (Seal of the Commander of the Zhenhai military zone)
Field Museum of Natural History, Chicago; no. 117065

19. (Pl. 50)
Buddhist Seal
Ming dynasty (1368-1644)
Bronze, 2 1/4 x 2 1/4 x 1 1/32 in. (5.8 x 5.8 x 2.6 cm)
Relief legend: *Fofaseng bao* (The [three Buddhist] treasures: Buddha, *dharma*, and the monastic order)
Field Museum of Natural History, Chicago; no. 117073

For a similar seal, see Luo Fuyi (1981a), 37.

20. (Pl. 48)
Zhou Bin (active late 17th c.)
Fisherman
Qing dynasty
Not engraved Shoushan stone, 1 3/4 x 2 1/4 x 1 in. (4.4 x 5.7 x 2.5 cm)
Wang Fang-yu and Sum Wai Wang

 Side inscription of No. 20

21. (Pl. 41)
Huang Yi (1744-1802)
Seal
Qing dynasty, dated 1777
Qingtian stone, 3/4 x 3/4 x 1 1/4 in. (1.9 x 1.9 x 3.2 cm)
Relief legend: *Wupiao shuhua* (Calligraphy and painting of Wupiao)
Yi Lei Wang

This seal has a side inscription by Wang Fu´an (1880-1960) dated 1946.

22. (Pl. 26)
Chen Hongshou (1768-1822; *hao* Mansheng)
Seal
Qing dynasty
Shoushan stone, 1 1/4 x 3/4 x 3/8 in. (3.2 x 1.9 x 1 cm)
Half-intaglio and half-relief legend: *Chen Mansheng*
Wang Fang-yu and Sum Wai Wang

The poem composed and inscribed on the side of the seal reads:

> These beautiful trees and flowers remind me
>   of what you have said before;
> This colorful landscape painting indicates that
>   we will meet again later in a similar
>   beautiful place.
>   (Trans. Wang Fang-yu)

23. (Pl. 42)
Zhao Zhichen (1781-1852; *zi* Cixian)
Seal
Qing dynasty, dated 1827
Qingtian stone, 1/2 x 1 x 1 in. (1.3 x 2.5 x 2.5 cm)
Relief legend: *Da jixiang* (Great auspiciousness)
Yi Lei Wang

24. (Pl. 29)
Wu Xizai (1799-1870)
Seal
Qing dynasty
Shoushan stone, 1 1/3 x 1 1/3 x 11/12 in.
  (3.4 x 3.4 x 2.3 cm)
Intaglio legend: *Shuxiang mendi* (Born to a literary
  family)
Yi Lei Wang

This seal has a side inscription by Wang Fu'an (1880-1960).

25. (Pl. 30)
Xu Sangeng (1806-1890)
Double-Sided Seal
Qing dynasty, dated 1885
Qingtian stone, 1 1/2 x 1 1/2 x 2 in. (3.8 x 3.8 x 5.1 cm)
Relief legend: *Dingsu*
Intaglio legend: *Jiehan moyuan* (To meet friend through
  brush and ink)
Yi Lei Wang

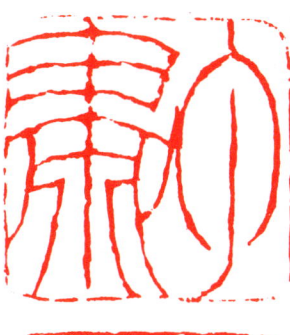

26. (Color pl. 5)
Qian Song (1807-1860; *zi* Shugai)
Seal
Qing dynasty
Shoushan stone, *tianhuang* type, height: 3 3/4 in. (9.5 cm)
Relief legend: *Xiangxue zhai cang* (In the collection of
  Xiangxue zhai)
On loan to The Brooklyn Museum from The Guennol
  Collection
Published: *The Guennol Collection*, vol. 3 (New York:
  The Brooklyn Museum, 1992), 110-111.

The sides of the stone are carved with a colophon by Qian Song and a scene depicting the excursion of the Song dynasty poet Su Shi to the Red Cliff.

27. (Pl. 32)
Zhao Zhiqian (1829-1884)
Pair of Seals
Shoushan stone
Qing dynasty
Height: 2 5/8 in. (6.7 cm) (each)
A. Relief legend: *Song ting* (Pine courtyard)
B. Intaglio legend: *Liu Xian zhiyin* (Seal of Liu Xian)
Robert Hatfield Ellsworth

79

28. (Color pl. 4; Pl. 51)
Huang Wenhan (active late 19th c.)
Double-Sided Seal
Qing dynasty, dated 1881
Ivory, height: 2 3/32 in. (5.3 cm)
Intaglio legend: *Huang Wenhan shici changshou yin* (Huang Wenhan's poetry is to have a long life)
Relief legend: *Yizhu ciguan zhuren shouzhu* (The master of the poetic studio for bowing to bamboo; slender bamboo)
Dr. Paul Singer

The remaining four sides are engraved as well. On one side is engraved a picture, "Bowing to Bamboo," based on the design of Qian Hui'an (1833-1911), a painter active in Shanghai.

On the side opposite to the picture is the side inscription by the seal engraver Yizhu Ciren (i.e. Huang Wenhan), who indicated that the seal was made in the *xinsi* year (1881) and that after he engraved the seal in the style of Han-dynasty seals, he asked Qian Hui´an to design the picture. He also inscribed a poem which reads:

> To love plum blossoms is my craving;
> To bow before stones is my craze.
> Craving, crazy:
> I wait on myself.

This poem is followed by yet another poem inscribed on another side:

> After getting drunk, I sing loudly;
> When I get unrestrained, I weep bitterly.
> It is only because we are full of emotions.

On the opposite side of the second poem an inscription from a Han-dynasty bronze basin is transcribed; the inscription reads:

> Great auspiciousness and prosperity
> appropriate for lords and princes.

29. (Pl. 61)
Double-Sided Seal in the Shape of an Ancient Coin
Probably Qing dynasty (1644-1912)
Soapstone, height: 11/16 in. (1.7 cm)
Intaglio legend: *Tianzhen* (Naturalness)
Relief legend: *Shoujing* (To maintain tranquillity)
Dr. Paul Singer

30. (Pl. 52)
Seal with Double Dragon
Qing dynasty (1644-1912)
Nephrite, 3 5/16 x 4 3/16 x 4 3/16 in. (8.5 x 10.6 x 10.6 cm)
Relief legend: *Jingmingyuan bao* (Treasure of the Garden of Tranquillity and Brightness)
The Metropolitan Museum of Art, New York; Gift of Heber R. Bishop, 1902

31. (Pl. 34)
Wu Changshuo (1844-1927)
Seal
Dated 1916
Height: 2 1/8 in. (5.5 cm)
Relief legend: *Ziyuan*
Professor and Mrs. Hans H. Frankel

The artist's side inscription indicates that it was engraved when he was 72.

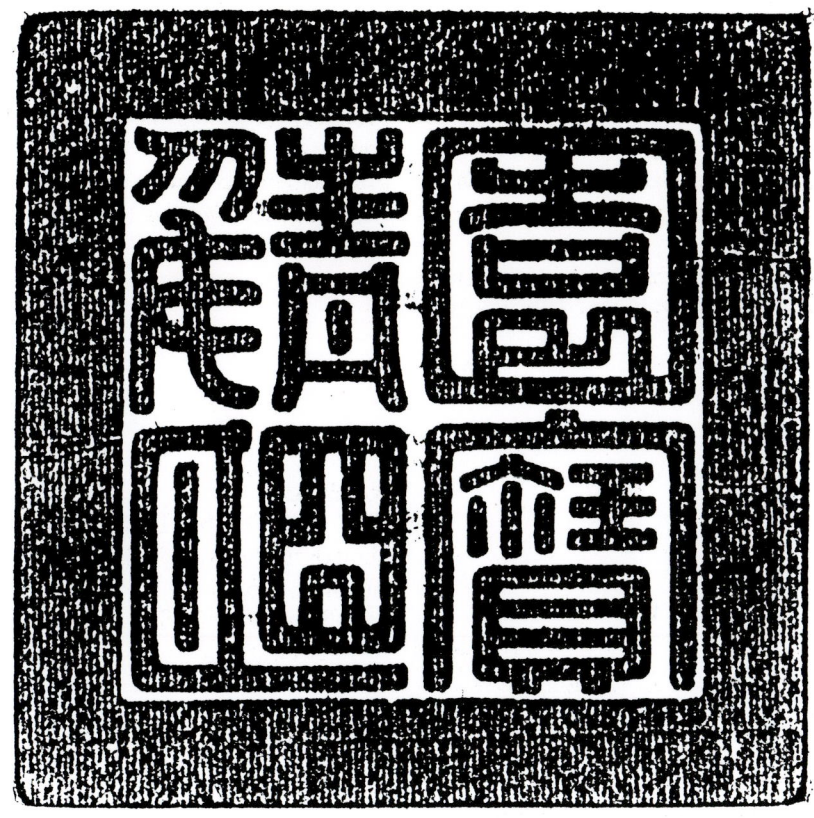

No. 30, rubbing of the seal legend showing the characters carved in reverse

32. (Pl. 33)
Wu Changshuo (1844-1927)
Seal
Qing dynasty, dated 1893
Shoushan stone, height: 1 1/2 in. (3.8 cm)
Relief legend: *Gaofeng*
Yi Lei Wang

33. (Pl. 33)
Wu Changshuo (1844-1927)
Seal
Qing dynasty, dated 1898
Qingtian stone, height: 1 3/4 in. (4.4 cm)
Relief legend: *Yipiao*
Yi Lei Wang

34. (Pl. 33)
Wu Changshuo (1844-1927)
Seal
Qing dynasty, dated 1898
Qingtian stone, height: 1 2/3 in. (4.2 cm)
Relief legend: *Zizi sunsun yongbaoyong* (To be treasured forever by sons and grandsons)
Yi Lei Wang

35. (Pl. 49)
Qi Baishi (1863-1957)
Seal
Shoushan stone, "white hibiscus" type, height: 2 3/4 in. (7 cm)
Relief legend: *Jing guan* (Watch carefully)
Wang Fang-yu and Sum Wai Wang
Published: Wang Fang-yu (1984), 19.

Back view of No. 35

36. (Pl. 38)
Qi Baishi (1863-1957)
Seal
Dated 1942
Qingtian stone, height: 2 1/4 in. (5.7 cm)
Relief legend: *Xunyun* (In search of clouds)
Yi Lei Wang

37. (Pl. 45)
Zhao Shuru (1874-1945)
Seal
Dated 1917
Shoushan stone, height: 2 1/4 in. (5.7 cm)
Relief legend: *Huade ziran* (Painting to achieve naturalness)
Yi Lei Wang

The top of the seal was carved by Zhou Bin, one of the most important carvers of seal knobs in the seventeenth century. His name was engraved in clerical script on the side of this seal.

38. (Pl. 44)
Zhao Guni (1875-1933)
Seal
Dated 1929
Shoushan stone, height: 2 1/4 in. (5.7 cm)
Relief legend: *Dai Zude*
Yi Lei Wang

39. (Pl. 46)
Tang Zuishi (1886-1969)
Seal
Dated 1947
Shoushan stone, height: 1 11/12 in. (4.9 cm)
Relief legend: *Xianyang jiuke* (A former sojourner at Xianyang)
Yi Lei Wang

40. (Pl. 47)
Pair of Seals
Qiao Dazhuang (1892-1948)
Shoushan stone, "white hibiscus" type, height: 1 3/4 in. (4.4 cm)
A. Relief legend: *Shiji zhilu* (The hut for eating chicken foot)
B. Intaglio legend: *Beiping Fangyu* (Fangyu from Beiping)
Wang Fang-yu and Sum Wai Wang
Published: Wang Fang-yu (1984), 18.

41. (Pl. 43)
Deng Sanmu
Seal
Dated 1938
Shoushan stone, diam.: 3/4 in. (1.9 cm)
Relief legend: *Mingyue dangtou* (Bright moon above the head)
Yi Lei Wang

BOOKS AND SEAL IMPRESSIONS

42. (Pl. 58)
Gu Congde (born ca. 1520), compiler
Jigu yinpu
Ming dynasty, dated 1575
Woodblock printed book of seal impressions,
    11 1/16 x 6 11/16 in. (28 x 17 cm)
Guanhai Lou Collection

This is probably the oldest extant book of seal impressions. It reproduced about 150 ancient jade seals and more than 1,600 ancient bronze seals from the Gu family collection and other contemporaneous collectors. The seal reproduced has an intaglio legend reading *Chenjichu yongkangxiu wanshouning* (Sickness cured, healthy forever, and live for ten thousand years in peace).

43. (Color pl. 3)
Hu Zhengyan (1584-1674), compiler
Yincun chuji
Qing dynasty, dated 1661
Woodblock printed book of seal impressions,
    10 1/4 x 6 1/2 x 1/2 in. (26.1 x 16.5 x 1.3 cm)
Wang Fang-yu and Sum Wai Wang

Hu Zhengyan (or Hu Yuecong) was one of the most important publishers in the 17th century. Among his major publications was *Shizhuzhai shuhuapu*, now in the collection of the Nelson-Atkins Museum of Art and the Cleveland Museum of Art (see Edgren and others, pp. 114-115).

44. (Pl. 60)
Wang Qishu (1728-1800), compiler
Feihongtang yinpu
Qing dynasty, dated 1776
Woodblock printed book of seal impressions
    (19th c. lithographic ed.), 10 3/8 x 6 x 7/16 in.
    (26.4 x 15.3 x 1.1 cm)
Gest Oriental Library and East Asian Collections,
    Princeton University, New Jersey

This book of seal impressions, prepared between 1745 and 1776, reproduced about 3,500 seals by Qing artists. Two seals are reproduced in this catalogue. The upper seal, by Wu Zhaojie, has an intaglio legend reading *Fuyun fuguei feisuoyuan* (Like floating cloud, I do not wish to attain wealth or honor). The lower seal is by Dong Xun (1740-1812); its relief legend reads *Jie mowu yu yunbian* (To make a thatched hut beside clouds). Dong Xun's seal engraving was inspired by He Zheng and Ding Jing. An accomplished seal engraver himself, the compiler, Wang Qishu was a bibliophile and avid collector of seals, including a large number of bronze seals of the Qin and Han dynasties. He published twenty-seven books of seal impressions.

45. (Pl. 57)
Chen Lian (1730-1778)
Shuyunlou yinpu
Qing dynasty, dated 1765
Woodblock printed book of seal impressions,
    10 1/16 x 6 1/2 in. (25.5 x 16.5 cm)
Guanhai Lou Collection

This is one of three books with seal impressions of seals engraved by the artist Chen Lian, who also compiled the books. This book reproduced 199 seals. Chen Lian's seal engraving improved after he studied thousands of Han and Qin seals in the collection of Wang Qishu, compiler of *Feihongtang yinpu*. The three seals reproduced here on two pages are *Peijingtang* (Hall of Nourishing Thorn or Bramble) inscribed in intaglio; *Wenqizhai tushuji*, inscribed in relief; and *Chuqingjing yi yangzhi* (To live in tranquillity in order to nourish one's feelings).

46. (Pl. 59)
Gu Xiang and Gu Hao (active early 19th c.), compilers
Xiaoshi shanfang yinpu
Qing dynasty, dated 1831
Woodblock printed book of seal impressions,
    7 5/8 x 5 x 3/8 in. (12.7 x 9.4 x 1 cm)
Gest Oriental Library and East Asian Collections,
    Princeton University, New Jersey

Gu Xiang was the father of Gu Hao. In addition to the *Xiaoshi shanfang yinpu*, the father-son team compiled the *Zhuanxue suozhu* (1840), a compendium of writings related to seal engraving by various authors since the Tang dynasty. In six volumes, the *Zhuanxue suozhu* reproduces seals from the compilers' collection, for a total of 346 seals by Ming and Qing artists. One of the supplemental volumes is devoted to a complete transcription of Tao Qian's (Tao Yuanming; 365-427) famous poem "Returning Home!" (*Guiqulai ci*) of 405, done with fifty-three seals that the compilers acquired in Suzhou.

The seal reproduced in this catalogue has an intaglio legend reading *Tianyuan jiangwu hubugui* (My fields and gardens will be covered with weeds, why not return?), taken from the first part of the poem which reads, in part:

> When I have made my heart the body's slave,
> Why should I sorrow and solitary grieve?
> Aware 'that the past may not be censured,'
> I know 'the future is to be striven for.'
> Truly I am not far astray from the road;
> I feel today is right, yesterday was wrong.
> My boat lightly tosses on the broad waters;
> The wind, whirling, blows my robe about.
> I ask a traveller of the way ahead;
> I resent the dawn light's faintness.
> Then I espy my humble house;
> So I am glad, so I run.
> The servants welcome me;
> The children wait at the gate.
>
> (Trans. Davis, 192)

47. (Color pl. 6)
Wu Xizai (1799-1870)
Wu Rangzhi yinpu
Qing dynasty, 19th century
Album of seal impressions,
    13 1/2 x 6 3/4 x 1 1/8 in. (34.3 x 17.2 x 2.9 cm)
Dr. Sesin Jong

The seals in this album are hand-impressed and accompanied by handwritten annotations and a colophon by Wu Xizai. The two seals reproduced in Color Plate 6C are: (at the top) a seal with a legend in relief, reading *Gudao caotang* (The thatched-hall for attracting the Tao); and (at the bottom) *Zhaowu jiangjun wushi sun Liang* (Liang: The fifth generation descendant of the General of Displaying Military Strength), also in relief.

48. (Pl. 27)
Anonymous
Portraits of Seal Artists
Qing dynasty, 19th century
Handscroll mounted as an album in 2 volumes,
    ink rubbing on paper, 11 3/4 x 5 1/4 x 1/4 in.
    (29.8 x 13.3 x .6 cm)
Wang Fang-yu and Sum Wai Wang

The album depicts a series of famous seal engravers. Here, in Plate 27, Wu Xizai is shown at the age of 72. A postscript by Hu Zongcheng dated 1861 follows.

49. (Pl. 13)
**"Shuowen jiezi" by Xu Shen with hand-written
    annotations by Wu Xizai**
Ming dynasty, 17th century
Woodblock printed book with hand-written notes in ink,
    11 1/4 x 7 1/4 x 1/4 in. (28.6 x 18.4 x .6 cm)
Wang Fang-yu and Sum Wai Wang

This Han dynasty dictionary, published by Mao Jin (1598-1659) in the seventeenth century, was the personal copy of Wu Xizai (1799-1870; *hao* Rangzhi), who wrote extensive comments in the upper margin in a fine, small regular script.

50. (Pl. 7)
Chen Jieqi (1813-1884), compiler
Shizhong shanfang yinju
Qing dynasty, first published 1872
Book of seal impressions, 8 1/2 x 5 3/16 x 3/16 in.
    (21.6 x 13.2 x .4 cm)
Gest Oriental Library and East Asian Collections,
    Princeton University, New Jersey.

Originally published in 1872 in a hundred volumes, then expanded in 1884 to 191 volumes, the entire work reproduced a total of 10,284 seals from the collections of Chen Jieqi himself and many other important collectors of his time such as Wu Dacheng (1835-1902), Wu Shifen, Wu Yun (1811-1883), and Li Zuoxian (*jinshi* 1835). Chen Jieqi was an important scholar and collector of ancient bronzes; some of his bronzes are now in the collection of the Freer Gallery of Art in Washington, D.C. (see Pope et al., 1: 308, 405).

The seal reproduced here has an intaglio legend reading *Huaiyangwang xi* (Seal of the Prince of Huaiyang).

51. (Pls. 8, 9)
Wu Shifen and Chen Jieqi, compilers
Fengni kaolüe
Qing dynasty, dated 1904
Lithographic printed book, 10 1/8 x 6 x 7/16 in.
    (25.8 x 15.3 x 1.1 cm)
Gest Oriental Library and East Asian Collections,
    Princeton University, New Jersey

This book reproduced clay sealings from the compilers' collections. Most of the clay sealings are from official seals of the Han dynasty. Good impressions are usually the result of intaglio rather than relief legends; when they were stamped on clay, they produced impressions with characters in relief. The impression pictured at the right reads *Dasikong yinzhang* (Pl. 9); that on the left reads *Qiangnu jiangjun* (Pl. 8).

Wu Shifen was a scholar of Chinese bronzes. His 1895 book, *Jungulu jinwen*, recorded the inscriptions of 1,334 bronzes.

52. (Pl. 14)
Wu Changshuo (1844-1927)
Handscroll of Seal Impressions
Ink on paper, 26 1/4 x 9 1/8 in. (66.7 x 23.2 cm)
Chien Lu Collection

The twenty-four impressions of seals engraved
    by Wu Changshuo read:

1. Top row, from right to left:

    A. *Anji Wu Jun zhang* (Seal of Wu Jun
        [i.e., Wu Changshuo] from Anji)
    B. *Huzhou Anjixian* (Wu Changshuo's birthplace)
    C. *Mingyue qianshen* (Reincarnation of the Moon
        [referring to Wu Changshuo's wife, who once
        appeared in the artist's dream;
        engraved in 1909])
    D. *Soushiting* (The pavilion for gathering stones)
    E. *Meiyi yannian* (Kind intention to wish
        for long life)
    F. *Shiyun shuhua* (Calligraphy and painting
        of Shiyun)
    G. *Xibi langgan hupuolong* (a quotation from
        Jijiu pian, a Han-dynasty primer for children)
    H. *Xuexinting* (Listening with one's heart
        eager to learn)

2. Middle row, from right to left:

    I. *Wuya* (The word *ya* refers to *huaya*, or *yazi*,
        which means "flourish signature," written in

cursive or running script in highly abbreviated form; this seal and No. 52Q below were carved together on a two-sided seal by Wu Changshuo in 1913.)
J. *Puohe* (Withered lotus)
K. *Wu Yü zhiyin* (This and No. 52S below were seals of Wu Changshuo's son Wu Yü, engraved in 1885.)
L. *Deshizhechang* (Those who seize the right moment will flourish and prosper.)
M. *Aiji zhigou* (I love my own fishing hook [a quotation from *Huainanzi*])
N. *Xiaojun* (Personal name)
O. *Meihua shouduan* (The power of plum blossom)
P. *Xiangsi dezhi* (This legend and No. 52X below were engraved on a double-sided seal; both were clearly inspired by Han seals.)

3. Bottom row, from right to left:

Q. *Fouweng* (Wu Changshuo's *hao*, meaning "An old man who loves a clay pot"; Wu Changshuo owned a pot with an impressed pattern, probably from the Warring States period.)
R. *Bichan* (The zen [or chan] of pottery [the artist's studio name, referring to his source of inspiration in ancient pottery])
S. *Bancang* (Personal name)
T. *Baoyuantian* (To embrace the round Heaven [a quotation from *Huainanzi*])
U. *Qiangqigu* (Strengthening the bones [a quotation from *Daodejing*])
V. *Gouyouxu* (Old women have whiskers [a quotation from *Xunzi*])
W. *Qiangyouer* (The walls have ears [a quotation from *Guanzi*])
X. *Rixinchangji* (Everyday is a renewal; long auspiciousness)

These impressions were made in 1980 by Wu Changye, grandson of Wu Changshuo. Several of the seals contain legends quoted from classical Chinese texts. For instance, the legend of Number 52U reads *Qiangqigu*, or "strengthening the bones," and comes from a passage in the *Daodejing*:

> Therefore in governing the people, the sage empties their minds but fills their bellies, weakens their wills but strengthens their bones. He always keeps them innocent of knowledge and free from desire, and ensures that the clever never dare to act.
> (Trans. D. C. Lau, 59)

Another classical reference is found in number 52V, *Gouyouxu*, or "old women have whiskers," which is from a passage in *Xunzi*:

> Mountains and abysses are level.
> Heaven and Earth are comparable.
> Qi and Qin are adjacent.
> Mountains issue out of mouths.
> Old women have whiskers.
> Eggs have feathers.

All these are theories that are difficult to uphold, yet Hui Shi and Deng Xi were capable of doing so. Nonetheless, the gentleman does not prize their feats of sophistry because they are contrary to the mean of behavior prescribed by ritual and moral principles.
(Trans. Knoblock, 1: 174)

The legend, *bichan* (No. 52R), or the *chan* of pottery, alludes to a passage in the Daoist text, *Zhuangzi*:

> Master Tung-kuo (Dongguo) asked Chuang Tzu (Zhuang Zi), "This thing call the Way—where does it exist?"
>
> Chuang Tzu said, "There's no place it doesn't exist."
>
> "Come," said Master Tung-kou, "you must be more specific!"
>
> "It is in the ant."
>
> "As low as that?"
>
> "It is in the panic grass."
>
> "But that's lower still!"
>
> "It is in the tiles and shards."
>
> "How can it be so low?"
>
> "It is in the piss and shit!"
>
> Master Tung-kuo made no reply.
> (Trans. Watson, 240-41)

53. (Pl. 37)
Qi Baishi (1863-1957) and others
Qi Baishi shoupi shisheng yinji
Book of seal impressions, 12 x 6 1/2 x 3/8 in.
 (30.5 x 16.5 x 1 cm)
Gest Oriental Library and East Asian Collections, Princeton University, New Jersey

Among the commentaries by Qi Baishi in this book is the following on his own seal with the intaglio legend *Wang Zhiqi yin* (Seal of Wang Zhiqi). It is reproduced here from part 1, vol. 1, p. 24, and it reveals his attitude toward antiquity:

> Vulgar people who carve seals like to say that they are following the seal engraving of the Qin and Han dynasties. In fact, they cannot even learn a tiny bit from the ancients. In seal engraving, I am always afraid that my seals look like Qin and Han seals. Yesterday my friend Chen Banding said that this seal looked exactly like the best seals from the Han dynasty because of my skills.

CALLIGRAPHY AND PAINTING

54. (Pl. 5)
Xu Lin (1462-1538)
**Frontispiece to "Autumn Mountain,"
by Wen Zhengming**
Handscroll, ink on gold-flecked paper, 12 1/2 x 47 1/2 in.
 (31.8 x 120.8 cm)
Artist's seal: *Xu Ziren shi* (intaglio legend)
The Art Institute of Chicago; Kate S. Buckingham Fund,
 1948.103
Published: Fu et al. (1977), fig. 29

The two boldly brushed characters in seal-script calligraphy reading *qiushan* (autumn mountain) refer to the subject of the handscroll by Wen Zhengming that follows. The calligrapher, Xu Lin, who was praised by his contemporaries for his seal script, purposely used dry ink to achieve a hatched effect, called *feibai* (flying white), at the bottom of the first character.

55. (Pl. 4)
Wu Yi (1472-1519)
Enjoying the Pines
Calligraphy frontispiece to anonymous, *Landscape
 in the style of Shen Zhou*
Handscroll, ink on gold-flecked paper, 12 1/2 x 35 1/4 in.
 (31.8 x 89.5 cm)
Artist's seal: *Siyefu yin* (relief legend)
The Metropolitan Museum of Art, New York;
 Bequest of John M. Crawford, Jr., 1988
Published: Wilson and Wong, no. 17

56. (Pl. 25)
Wen Peng (1498-1573)
Draft Poem for Seeing Off Lin Jun
Ming dynasty, datable to 1523
Large album leaf, ink on paper, 11 1/8 x 15 5/8 in.
 (28.3 x 39.7 cm)
Artist's seals: *Wen Peng yin* (half relief and half
  intaglio); *Wen Shoucheng fu* (relief)
The Metropolitan Museum of Art, New York;
 Bequest of John M. Crawford, Jr., 1988
Published: Wilson and Wong (1974), no. 22

57. (Pl. 28)
Wu Xizai (1799-1870)
Transcription of "The Book of Songs"
Set of four hanging scrolls, ink on paper, 51 1/2 x 12 in.
 (130.8 x 30.5 cm) (each)
Artist's seals: *Wu Xizai yin* (intaglio legend)
  Rangzhi (relief legend)
F. Randall and Judith G. Smith

The poem reads:

On the southern hills grows the nutgrass;
On the northern hills the goosefoot.
Happiness to our lord
That is the groundwork of land and home!
Happiness to our lord!
May he live for evermore.

On the southern hills the mulberry;
On the northern hills the willow.
Happiness to our lord,
That is the light of land and home.
Happiness to our lord!
May he live for ever and ever.

On the southern hills the aspen;
On the northern hills the plum-tree.
Happiness to our lord
That is the father and mother of his people.
Happiness to our lord!
May his fair fame be forever.
On the southern hills the cedrela;
On the northern hills the privet.
Happiness to our lord,
Yes, and life long-lasting!
Happiness to our lord!
May his fair fame never droop.

On the southern hills the box-thorn;
On the northern hills the catalpa.
Happiness to our lord,
Yes, till looks are seer and face is grey!
Happiness to you, our lord!
To your descendants, safety and peace!
 (Trans. Waley 1960, p. 179)

58. (Color pl. 7)
Wu Xizai (1799-1870)
Apricot
Fan painting, ink and color on alum paper,
 7 3/8 x 21 1/2 in. (18.8 x 54.7 cm)
Artist's seal: *Wu Xizai* (intaglio legend)
The Metropolitan Museum of Art, New York;
 Gift of Robert Hatfield Ellsworth in memory of
 La Ferne Hatfield Ellsworth, 1986
Published: Ellsworth 2: 22

59. (Pl. 31)
He Shaoji (1799-1873)
Couplet in Seal Script
Qing dynasty, 19th century
Pair of hanging scrolls, 51 x 11 3/4 in.
 (129.6 x 29.9 cm) (each)
Artist's seals: *He Shaoji* (relief legend);
  Zizhen (intaglio legend)
Chien Lu Collection

The seven-character couplet reads:

> Ten miles of mist and waves—
> > the bright moon night;
> Ten thousand songs in concord—
> > the early spring sky.

60. (Color pl. 8)
Zhao Zhiqian (1829-1884)
Calligraphy in Seal Script
Qing dynasty, dated 1867
Pair of hanging scrolls, ink on paper, 72 x 19 in.
 (182.9 x 48.3 cm)
Artist's seal: *Zhao Zhiqian yin* (intaglio legend)
F. Randall and Judith G. Smith

The five-character couplet reads:

> Because one has forbearance, one's virtue is
> > thus great.
> Because one does not deceive, one's thoughts
> > are naturally sincere.

61. (Color pl. 9)
Xu Sangeng (1826-1890)
Meet the Plum and Moon by Chance
Qing dynasty, dated 1887
Seal-script calligraphy
Pair of hanging scrolls, ink on paper, 52 1/2 x 12 1/2 in.
(133.4 x 31.8 cm) (each)
Artist's seals: *Xu Sangeng yin* (Seal of Xu Sangeng)
 (intaglio legend); *Xiuhai* (*hao* of Xu
 Sangeng) (relief legend); *Xueran sanren*
 (*hao* of Xu Sangeng) (relief legend)
Robert Hatfield Ellsworth
Published: Ellsworth, 3: 92

The seven-character couplet reads:

> Meet the plum and moon by chance when
> > walking in the mountains.
> Cover the world with grass, and plant orchids
> > beside the rock.
> > > (Trans. Ellsworth, 1: 258)

The postscript-dedication reads:

> At the request of Wuyun, I have written these lines
> in the style of Huangxiang's calligraphic style.

Huangxiang is the purported artist of *Tianfa shenchenbei*, dated 276, which has been a major source of inspiration for later calligraphers and seal engravers (*SZ*, vol. 3, pls. 77-82).

62. (Pl. 3)
Wu Changshuo (1844-1927)
After the Ten Stone Drums Inscription
Dated 1925
Hanging scroll, 52 x 25 in. (132.1 x 63.5 cm)
Artist's seals: *Wu Junqing* (intaglio legend), *Changshuo*
 (intaglio legend)
Dr. and Mrs. Clyde Wu

The artist gave an abbreviated transcription of the original text, which is only partially understood by scholars and which reads (the letters X, Y, and Z in the following translation refer to points that are not understood by scholars):

> The Qian X flows amply.
> Magnificent is that miry abyss.
> The mud-fish and carp inhabit it,
> And the noblemen fish it.
>
> In the shallows are small fish;
> Their swimming is in schools.
> The white fish shimmer;
> Their abundance is most rare.
> Yellow and white are the bream.
>
> There are *fang*-bream, there are *bai*-cutler.
> Their silhouettes are ever so numerous.
> The X-ing (netting?) of them is X-ly,
> It is Y-ly and Z-ly.
>
> What are its fishes?
> They are tench, they are carp.
> With what should we wrap them?
> Let it be [the branches of] the poplar
> > and willow.
> > > (Trans. Mattos, 195-196)

63. (Pl. 40)
Zhao Shuru (1874-1945)
Calligraphy in Seal Script
Dated 1935
Pair of hanging scrolls, ink on gold-flecked paper,
 67 1/4 x 9 3/8 in. (170.8 x 23.8 cm) (each)
Artist's seals: *Yihai* (1935) (relief legend); *Zhao Shigang
 yin* (Seal of Zhao Shuru) (relief legend);
 Chijin Zhaoshi zhixi (Seal of Mr. Zhao
 from Chijin) (intaglio legend)
Robert Hatfield Ellsworth
Published: Ellsworth, 3: 192

The nine-character couplet reads:

> The fish and birds of the Hao and Pu Rivers
> > enjoyed their leisure.
> The eccentric rock and bamboo are like the
> > people of Wei and Jin times.
> > > (Trans. Ellsworth, 1: 330)

64. (Pl. 35)
Qi Baishi (1863-1957)
If You Have a Relaxed Attitude
Datable to 1948
Seal-script calligraphy
Album leaf, ink on paper, 12 1/2 x 12 1/2 in.
    (31.8 x 31.8 cm)
Artist's seal: *Baishi weng* (Old man Baishi) (relief
    legend)
Robert Hatfield Ellsworth
Published: Ellsworth, 3: 214

The inscribed poem contains four lines with seven characters in each line:

> If you have a relaxed attitude toward your work,
>   everything will become easy.
> The flying bird that departs in the morning
>   returns at evening.
> The message was sent to remote Heshang
>   with the gods' help.
> Admiring you standing by the pass of
>   Guyi Mountain.
>   (Trans. Ellsworth, 1: 339)

The postscript reads:

> My teacher [Wang] Xiangqi has rated this poem in the
> first rank among *jueju* poems from the Tang dynasty.

65. (Pl. 36)
Qi Baishi (1863-1957)
Snow Claw
Datable to 1953
Album leaf, ink on paper, 12 1/8 x 7 1/4 in.
    (30.8 x 18.4 cm)
Artist's seal: *Jiushier weng* (92-year-old man)
    (intaglio legend)
Robert Hatfield Ellsworth
Published: Ellsworth, 3: 219

The two large seal-script characters, "snow claw," refer to the transcience of human affairs, like the footprints of geese in the snow.

66. (Pl. 39)
Huang Binhong (1864-1955)
In Describing Rocks
Pair of hanging scrolls, ink on paper, 59 3/4 x 10 3/8 in.
    (151.8 x 26.4 cm) (each)
Artist's seals: *Bingshang hongfei guan* (Studio of Geese
    Flying over Ice) (relief legend); *Huang Zhi
    Binhong* (Binhong is the *hao* of Huang
    Zhi) (intaglio legend); *Huangshan
    shanzhongren* (The man who lives in Mt.
    Huang) (relief legend)
Robert Hatfield Ellsworth
Published: Ellsworth, 3: 210

The seven-character couplet in seal-script calligraphy reads:

> In describing rocks, Guo Youdao has a lofty
>   reputation.
> In painting plums, Wang Yuanzhang has been
>   followed by all.

Wang Yuanzhang is Wang Mian (1287-1359), painter and seal engraver.

ACCESSORIES OF THE SEAL ENGRAVER

67. (Pl. 55)
Seal Paste and Seal-Paste Box
20th century
Mixture of oils and pigments in a porcelain container,
    diameter: 3 1/4 in. (8.3 cm.)
Private collection

68. (Pl. 53)
Set of Carving Knives
20th century
Ten steel knives with various blades each wrapped
    in string, length: 6 1/4 in. (16.1 cm.) (each)
Private collection

69. (Pl. 54)
Seal Clamp
20th century
Wooden clamp with removable slats,
    2 1/4 x 6 1/2 x 3 in. (5.8 x 16.6 x 7.7 cm.)
Private collection

70. (Pl. 56)
Seal Paste Box
Qing dynasty (1644-1912)
Nephrite, 4 7/8 x 3 3/4 x 3 3/4 in. (12.4 x 9.5 x 9.5 cm)
The Metropolitan Museum of Art, New York;
    Gift of Heber R. Bishop, 1902

REFERENCE LIST

Abbreviations

CTS: Kobayashi, *Chūgoku tenkoku sōkan*

LS: *Lidai shufa lunwenxuan*

LY: Han Tianheng, *Lidai yinxue lunwenxuan*

SP: *Shupu* (periodical)

SZ: *Shodō zenshū*

ZMQ: *Zhongguo meishu quanji*

ZMZ: *Zhongguo meixueshi ziliao xuanbian*

A Cheng. "Line." Translated by Barbara Shen and Richard Buchanan. *Design Issues* 7, no. 2 (Spring 1991): 5-16.

Addis, Stephen, et al. *Calligraphy of China and Japan: The Grand Tradition*. Ann Arbor: University of Michigan Museum of Art, 1975.

Arnheim, Rudolf. *Toward a Psychology of Art: Collected Essays*. Berkeley and Los Angeles: University of California Press, 1966.

Barnhart, Richard. "Wei Fu-jen's *Pi Chen T'u* and the Early Texts on Calligraphy." *Archives of the Chinese Art Society of America* 18 (1964), pp. 13-25.

————. "Chinese Calligraphy: The Inner World of the Brush." *Metropolitan Museum of Art Bulletin* 30, no. 5 (1972): 230-41.

————. "Reading the Paintings and Calligraphy of Bada Shanren." In *Master of the Lotus Garden: The Life and Art of Bada Shanren (1626-1705)*, by Wang Fang-yu and Richard Barnhart, 83-216. New Haven: Yale University Art Gallery, 1990.

Beijing tushuguan, ed. *Qi Baishi shoupi shisheng yinji*. Beijing: Shumu wenxian chubanshe, 1987.

Bennett, Elizabeth Foard. "Chao Chih-ch'ien (1929-1884), A Late Nineteenth Century Chinese Artist: His Life, Calligraphy and Painting." Ph. D. dissertation, Yale University, 1983.

Billeter, Jean Francois. *The Chinese Art of Writing*. Translated by Jean-Marie Clarke and Michael Taylor. New York: Rizzoli International Publications, 1990.

Bodde, Derk. *Chinese Thought, Society, and Science*. Honolulu: University of Hawaii, 1991.

Bothwell, Dorr and Mayfield, Marlys. *Notan: The Dark-Light Principle of Design*. New York: Dover Publications, 1991.

Burling, Judith and Arthur Hart Burling. "Seals on Chinese Painting." *Apollo* 48, no. 286 (December 1948): 144-48.

Cahill, James. "Style as Idea in Ming-Ch'ing Painting." In *The Mozartian Historian: Essays on the Works of Joseph R. Levenson*, ed. Maurice Meisner and Rhodes Murphey, 137-56. Berkeley: University of California Press, 1976.

Chang, Kwang-chih. *Shang Civilization*. New Haven and London: Yale University Press, 1980.

Chang, Leon Long-yien and Miller, Peter. *Four Thousand Years of Chinese Calligraphy*. Chicago and London: University of Chicago Press, 1990

Chaves, Jonathan. "The Legacy of Ts'ang Chieh: The Written Word as Magic." *Oriental Art*, n.s. 23, no. 2 (Summer 1977): 200-215.

Ch'en, Chih-mai. *Chinese Calligraphers and Their Art*. London and New York: Cambridge University Press, 1966.

Chen Zizhuang. *Shihu lunhua yuyao*. Compiled by Chen Zidong. Chengdu: Sichuan meishu chubanshe, 1987.

Cheng Te-k'un. *Studies in Chinese Art*. Hong Kong: Chinese University Press, 1983.

Chiang Yee. *Chinese Calligraphy*. 3rd rev. ed. Cambridge: Harvard University Press, 1973.

Coleman, Earle J. *Philosophy of Painting by Shih T'ao: A Translation and Exposition of his "Hua-P'u."* The Hague and Paris: Mouton Publishers, 1978.

Contag, Victoria, and C. C. Wang. *Seals of Chinese Painters and Collectors of the Ming and Ch'ing Periods.* Rev. ed. with supplement. Hong Kong: Hong Kong University Press, 1966.

Dai Lin. *Zhongguo yinzhang yishu.* Beijing: Meishu sheyin chubanshe, 1990.

Davis, A. R. *Tao Yuan-ming (AD 365-427): His Works and Their Meaning.* 2 vols. Cambridge: Cambridge University Press, 1983.

Deng Sanmu. *Zhuankexue.* Beijing: Renmin meishu chubanshe, 1979.

Dondis, Donis A. *A Primer of Visual Literacy.* Cambridge, Mass.: MIT Press, 1973.

Driscoll, Lucy, and Kenji Toda. *Chinese Calligraphy.* Chicago: University of Chicago, 1935.

Earnshaw, Christopher J. *Shō: Japanese Calligraphy.* Tokyo: Charles E. Tuttle, 1988.

Ecke, Tseng Yu-ho. *Chinese Calligraphy.* Philadelphia: Philadelphia Museum of Art, 1971.

Edgren, Sören, et al. *Chinese Rare Books in American Collections.* New York: China House Gallery, China Institute in America, 1985.

Edwards, Richard. "The Importance of Seals in Chinese Painting." In *The Collectors of Asian Art and Archaeology,* Asian Conservation Laboratory, 79-83. N.p., [1963].

—————. *The World Around the Chinese Artist.* Ann Arbor: University of Michigan, 1987.

Ehrenwerth, Diana. "Die Xiling Siegelgesellschaft in Hangzhou." Ph. D. dissertation, University of Vienna, 1988.

Ellsworth, Robert H. *Later Chinese Painting and Calligraphy, 1800-1950.* 3 vols. New York: Random House, 1987.

Elman, Benjamin A. *From Philosophy to Philology: Intellectual and Social Aspects of Change in Late Imperial China.* Cambridge, Mass.: Council on East Asian Studies, Harvard University, 1984.

Fang Jiekan. *Xiyin wenzong.* Shanghai: Shanghai shudian, 1989.

Fang Qiji. *Ming Qing zhuanke liupai yinpu.* Shanghai: Shanghai shuhua chubanshe, 1980.

Farquhar, David. "The Official Seals and Ciphers of the Yuan Period." *Monumenta Serica* 25 (1966): 169-96.

Fazzioli, Edoardo. *Chinese Calligraphy: From Pictograph to Ideogram.* Translated by Geoffrey Culverwell. New York: Abbeville Press, 1987.

Feng Zuomin. *Zhongguo yinpu.* Taipei: Yishu tushu gongsi, 1990.

Fong, Wen C. "Archaism as a 'Primitive' Style." In *Artists and Traditions: Uses of the Past in Chinese Culture,* edited by Christian F. Murck, 89-109. Princeton: The Art Museum, Princeton University, 1976.

—————, ed. *The Great Bronze Age of China.* New York: The Metropolitan Museum of Art, 1980.

—————. "The Modern Chinese Art Debate." Unpublished paper, 1989.

Fry, Roger. "The Significance of Chinese Art." In *Chinese Art: An Introductory Handbook to Painting, Sculpture, Ceramics, Textiles, Bronzes and Minor Arts* by Roger Fry, et al., 1-5. London: B. T. Batsford, Ltd., 1935.

Fu, Pao-shih. "Ch'i Pai-shih's Seal-engraving." *Chinese Literature,* No. 6 (1961), 127-134.

Fu, Shen C. Y. et al. *Traces of the Brush: Studies in Chinese Calligraphy.* New Haven: Yale University Art Gallery, 1977.

—————. "Huang Binhong's Shanghai Period Landscape Paintings and His Late Floral Works in the Arthur M. Sackler Gallery." *Orientations* 18, no. 9 (September 1987): 66-78.

Fu, Shen C. Y., Glenn D. Lowry, and Ann Yonemura. *From Concept to Context: Approaches to Asian and Islamic Calligraphy.* Washington, D. C.: Freer Gallery of Art, 1986.

Gaur, Albertine. *A History of Writing.* London: The British Library, 1987.

Gu Xiang, comp. *Zhuanxue congshu.* 2 vols. Reprint of *Zhuanxue suozhu,* preface dated 1843. Beijing: Zhongguo shudian, 1984.

Gulik, R. H. van, 1958a. *Chinese Pictorial Art as Viewed by the Connoisseur.* Rome: Is. M. E. O., 1958.

—————, 1958b. *Scrapbook for Chinese Collectors: A Chinese Treatise on Scrolls and Forgers, Shu-hua-shuoling.* Beirut: Imprimerie Catholique, 1958.

Han Tianheng. *Zhongguo zhuanke yishu*. Shanghai: Shanghai shuhua chubanshe, 1980.

―――, ed. *Lidai yinxue wenxuan*. 2 vols. Hangzhou: Xiling yinshe, 1985.

―――. *Zhongguo yinxue nianbiao*. Shanghai: Shanghai shuhua chubanshe, 1987.

―――. "Shanghai Gushi jigu yinpu chuyi." *Shufa yanjiu*, no. 42 (April 1990): 61-66.

Hattori, Kōseki. *Tenkoku jirin*. [Tokyo]: Shibundō shoten, 1927.

Hay, John. "The Human Body as Microcosmic Source of Macrocosmic Values in Calligraphy." In *Theories of Art in China*, edited by Susan Bush and Christian Murck, 74-104. (Princeton: Princeton University Press, 1983).

―――. *Kernels of Energy, Bones of Earth: The Rock in Chinese Art*. New York: China House Gallery, China Institute in America, 1986.

Hou Fuchang. *Niaochongshu huibian*. Taipei: Taiwan shangwu yinshuguan, 1990.

Hsu, Cho-yun, and Katheryn M. Linduff. *Western Chou Civilization*. New Haven and London: Yale University Press, 1988.

Huangshi Laoren. *Zhongguo yinpu jixuan*. Taipei: Xingguang chubanshe, 1984.

Huot, Marie-Claire. *Traduction, analyse, et commentaire du "Shuduan" (727) de Zhang Huaiguan (actif circa 713-760)*. Ph.D. dissertation, University of Montreal, 1986.

Jao, Tsung-i. "The Formal and Rhythmic Elements in Chinese Calligraphy." *Orientations* 21, no. 7 (July 1990): 54-65.

Jiaguwenbian, compiled by Institute of Archaeology, Chinese Academy of Sciences. Beijing: Zhonghua shuju, 1965.

Jiang Yisheng. *Zhuanke qiantan*. Hefei: Anhui renmin chubanshe, 1984.

Kang Yin. *Gu tuxing xiyin hui*. Hong Kong: Boyazhai, 1981.

Keightley, David N. "The Origins of Writing in China: Scripts and Cultural Contexts." In *The Origins of Writing*, edited by Wayne M. Senner, 171-202. (Lincoln and London: University of Nebraska Press, 1989).

King, Lynn. "Chinese Seals and Their Place in Chinese Painting." In *C. C. Wang: Landscape Painting*, with introduction by James Cahill, 71-75. N.p.: Hsi An T'ang, 1986.

Knoblock, John. *Xunzi: A Translation and Study of the Complete Works*. Stanford: Stanford University Press, 1988.

Ko Kan jiten. Kyoto: Mitsumura suiko shoten, 1984.

Kobayashi Toan, ed. *Chūgoku tenkoku sōkan*. 40 vols. Tokyo: Nigensha showa, 1981-84.

Kuo, Jason C. *Chinese Calligraphy in Michigan Private Collections: A Scholarly Review*. Ann Arbor: Chinese American Educational and Cultural Center of Michigan, [1987].

―――, 1989a. "Hui-chou Merchants as Art Patrons in the Late Sixteenth and Early Seventeenth Centuries." In *Artists and Patrons: Some Social and Economic Aspects of Chinese Painting*, edited by Chu-tsing Li, 177-188. Lawrence: The Kress Foundation Department of Art History, University of Kansas; Kansas City: The Nelson-Atkins Museum of Art, in association with University of Washington Press, Seattle and London, 1989.

―――, 1989b. *Innovation within Tradition: The Painting of Huang Pin-hung*. Williamstown: Williams College Museum of Art in association with Hanart Gallery, 1989.

―――. *The Austere Landscape: The Paintings of Hung-jen*. Taipei: SMC Publishing Inc., in cooperation with University of Washington Press, Seattle and London, 1991.

Kwo, Da-wei. *Chinese Brushwork: Its History, Aesthetics, and Techniques*. Montclair: Allanheld & Schram, 1981.

Lai, T. C. *Chinese Seals*. Seattle and London: University of Washington Press, 1976.

Lau, D. C., trans. *Tao Te Ching*. New York: Penguin Books, 1963.

Ledderose, Lothar. *Die Siegelschrift (Chuan-shu) in der Ch'ing-Zeit: Ein Beitrag zur Geschichte der chinesischen Schriftkunst*. Wiesbaden: Franz Steiner, 1970.

―――. "An Approach to Chinese Calligraphy." *National Palace Museum Bulletin* 7, no. 1 (1972): 1-14.

―――. "Chinese Calligraphy: Its Aesthetic Dimension and Social Function." *Orientations* 17, no. 10 (October 1986): 35-50.

———. "Chinese Calligraphy: Art of the Elite." In *World Art: Theme of Unity in Diversity*, edited by Irving Lavin. Acts of the 25th International Congress of the History of Art, 2: 291-294. University Park: Pennsylvania State University Press, 1989.

Lee, Sherman, and Waikam Ho. "The Nature and Significance of the Collection of Liang Ch'ing-piao." In *Proceedings of the International Conference on Sinology: Section of History of Art*, 101-157. Taipei: Academia Sinica, 1980.

Legeza, Laszlo. *Tao Magic: The Secret Language of Diagrams and Calligraphy*. London: Thames and Hudson, 1975.

Li, Chu-tsing, and James C. Y. Watt, eds. *The Chinese Scholar's Studio: Artistic Life in the Late Ming Period*. New York: The Asia Society Galleries, 1987.

Li Dongwan. "Lüelun Qin Han yinzhang di yishu fengge." *Shufa congkan*, no. 17 (February 1989): 86-91.

Li Guojun, ed. *Zhongguo shufa zhuanke dacidian*. [Changsha], Hunan: Hunan jiaoyu chubanshe, 1990.

Li Jian. *Jinshi zhuanke yanjiu*. Shanghai: Zhongguo lianhe chuban gongsi, 1943.

Li Qingye. *Zhuanfa chubu*. Luoyang: Henan renmin chubanshe, 1984.

Li, Shuhua. "The Early Development of Seals and Rubbings." *Tsing Hua Journal of Chinese Studies*, n.s. 1, no. 3 (1958): 61-87.

Li, T. K. "Chinese Seals." *Journal of the Royal Asiatic Society-Hong Kong Branch* 2 (1962): 49-53.

Li Xueqin. *Eastern Zhou and Qin Civilizations*. Translated by K. C. Chang. New Haven and London: Yale University Press, 1985.

Lidai shufa lunwenxuan. 2 vols. Shanghai: Shanghai Shuhua chubanshe, 1979.

Lin Hongyuan, ed. *Zhongguo shufa dazidian*. Rev. ed. Hong Kong: Zhongwai chubanshe, 1976.

Lin Suqing. *Zhuanke*. Taipei: Youshi wenhua shiye gongsi, 1986.

Lin, Yutang. *The Wisdom of China and India*. New York: Random House, 1942.

Lindqvist, Cecilia. *China: Empire of Living Symbols*. New York: Addison Wesley, 1989.

Liu Jiang. *Zhuanke yishu*. Hangzhou: Zhejiang meishu xueyuan chubanshe, 1988.

———. *Zhuanke jifa*. Hangzhou: Xiling yinshe, 1989.

Liu Zhenying. *Zhuanke qimeng yu jifa*. Beijing: Tiyu xueyuan chubanshe, 1989.

Luo Fuyi. "Cong yinzhang shang jianpie gushuhua." In *Zhongguo shuhua jianding yanjiu*, 114-128. Hong Kong: Nantong tushu gongsi, 1974.

———, 1981a. *Guxiyin gailun*. Beijing: Wenwu chubanshe, 1981.

———, 1981b. *Guxi wenbian*. Beijing: Wenwu chubanshe, 1981.

———, 1981c. *Guxi huibian*. Hong Kong: Zhonghua shuju, 1981.

———, 1982a. *Gugong bowuyuan cang guxiyin xuan*. Beijing: Wenwu chubanshe, 1982.

———, 1982b. *Jin bainianlai dui guxiyin yanjiu zhi fazhan*. Hangzhou: Xiling yinshe, 1982.

Luo Fuyi and Wang Rencong. *Yinzhang gaishu*. Hong Kong: Zhonghua shuju, 1973.

Luo Shibai. *Zenyang zhiyin*. Beijing: Renmin meishu chubanshe, 1962.

Luo Suizu. "Shilun Mi Fu di shuhua yongyin." *Shufa congkan*, no. 15 (September 1988): 92-96.

Ma Guoquan. "Xu sangeng hetade zhuanke yishu." *Xiling yiye*, no. 15 (July 1987): 1-8.

Mattos, Gilbert Louis. *The Stone Drums of Ch'in*. Nettetal: Steyler Verlag-Wort und Werk, 1988.

Meggs, Philip B. *Type and Image: The Language of Graphic Design*. New York: Van Nostrand Reinhold, 1989.

Ming Qing zhuankexuan. Shanghai: Shanghai shuhua chubanshe, 1984.

Moss, Paul. *The Literai Mode: Chinese Scholar Paintings, Calligraphy, and Desk Objects*. London: Sydney L. Moss Ltd., 1986.

Mote, Frederick W., and Hung-lam Chu. *Calligraphy and the East Asian Book*. Edited by Howard L. Goodman. Boston and Shaftesbury: Shambhala, 1989.

Mu Xiaotian and Xu Jiaqiong. *Deng Shiru*. Hefei: Anhui jiaoyu chubanshe, 1983.

———. *Deng Shiru yanjiu ziliao*. Beijing: Renmin meishu chubanshe, 1988.

Na, Zhiliang. "Xiang Zijing jiqi yinzhang." *Dalu zazhi* 13, no. 8 (October 1956): 258-62.

———. *Xiyin tongshi*. Taipei: Commercial Press, 1970.

———. *The Panoramic Views of Chinese Seal Development*. Taipei: China Cultural Enterprises, 1972.

Nakata, Yūjirō. *Chinese Calligraphy*. Translated and adapted by Jeffrey Hunter. New York and Tokyo: Weatherhill/Tankosha, 1983.

———, comp. *Nihon no tenkoku*. Tokyo: Nigensha, 1966.

National Palace Museum. *Masterpieces of Chinese Seals in the National Palace Museum*. Taipei: National Palace Museum, 1974.

Neill, Mary Gardner, et al. *The Communion of Scholars: Chinese Art at Yale*. New York: China House Gallery, China Institute in America, 1982.

Ogino Minahiko. *Inshō*. Tokyo: Yoshikawa kobunkan, 1966.

Palmer, Mildred. *A Chinese Seal, and Other Poems*. Philadelphia: Dorrance, 1923.

Pan Gongkai, ed. *Pan Tianshou tanyilu*. Hangzhou: Zhejiang renmin meishu chubanshe, 1985.

Pan Tianshou, *Lunhua bilu*. Compiled by Ye Shangqing. Shanghai: Renmin meishu chubanshe, 1984.

Pope, John Alexander, et al. *The Freer Chinese Bronzes*. 2 vols. Smithsonian Institution, Freer Gallery of Art, Oriental Studies, no. 7. Washington, D.C.: The Freer Gallery of Art, 1967.

Powers, Martin J. "Gesture in Early Chinese Art and Criticism." Abstract in *International Colloquium on Chinese Art, 1991*, 162-63. Taipei: National Palace Museum, 1991.

Qi Baishi shufa zhuanke. Beijing: Renmin meishu chubanshe, 1987.

Qian Juntao and Ye Luyuan. *Zhongguo xiyin yuanliu*. Hong Kong: Shanghai shuju, 1963.

Qinshihuang jinshi keci zhu. Shanghai: Renmin chubanshe, 1975.

Rong Geng, comp. *Jinwenbian*, 3rd ed. Beijing: Kexue chubanshe, 1959.

Shaughnessy, Edward L. *Sources of Western Zhou History: Inscribed Bronze Vessels*. Berkeley and Los Angeles: University of California Press, 1991.

Sha Menghai. *Yinxueshi*. Hangzhou: Xiling yinshe, 1987.

Shōdo zenshū. 28 vols. Tokyo: Heibonsha, 1954-68.

Shufa xiaocidian. Beijing: Beijing chubanshe, 1988.

Shuhua zhuanke shiyong cidian. Shanghai: Shanghai shuhua chubanshe, 1988.

Song, Shouquan, trans. "Letters and Inscriptions [by] Zheng Banqiao (1693-1765)." *Chinese Literature* (Spring 1984): 160-68.

Sun, Ta-yü. "On the Fine Art of Chinese Calligraphy by Sun Kuo-t'ing of the T'ang Dynasty." *T'ien Hsia Monthly* 1, no. 2 (Sept. 1935): 192-207.

Suzuki, Kei. "Siyin sankao." Translated by Wei Meiyue. *Gugong wenwu yuekan*, no. 97 (April 1991): 34-39.

Takata Chūshū. *Kochū hen*. 1925. Reprint. Taipei: Hongye shuju, 1975.

Tanguchi, Nishu. *Tenkoku: The Seal Engraving*. Tokyo: Japan Publications Trading Co., 1964.

Tseng, Yu-ho. *Some Contemporary Elements in Chinese Art*. Honolulu: University of Hawaii Press, 1963.

Tsien, Tsuen-hsuin. *Written on Bamboo and Silk: The Beginnings of Chinese Books and Inscriptions*. Chicago: University of Chicago Press, 1962.

———. *Paper and Printing*. In *Science and Civilization in China*, edited by Joseph Needham, vol. 5, pt. 1. Cambridge: Cambridge University Press, 1985.

Uyehara, Cecil H. *Japanese Calligraphy: A Bibliographical Study*. Lanham: University Press of America, 1991.

Veit, Willibald. *Siegel und Siegelschrift der Chou-, Ch'in- und Han-Dynastie*. Ph. D. dissertation, University of Cologne, 1977. Wiesbaden: Franz Steiner, 1985.

Wagner, Lothar. "Chinesische Siegel. Ein kurzer Überblick." *Ruperto Carola*, nos. 65-66 (September 1981): 132-46.

———. "Die ganze Welt in einem Zoll. Ein Beitrag zur chinesischen Siegelkunde." Ph. D. dissertation, University of Heidelberg, 1987.

———. *Kunst und Geschichte des chinesischen Siegels. Eine Einführung.* Bonn: J. Latka Verlag. Forthcoming.

Waley, Arthur. *The Way and Its Power: A Study of the Tao Te Ching and Its Place in Chinese Thought.* New York: Grove Press, 1958.

———, trans. *The Book of Songs.* New York: Grove Press, 1960.

Wang Beiyue. *Zhuanke shuyao.* Taipei: Zhonghua congshu bianshen weiyuanhui, 1977.

Wang Beiyue. *Zhuanke yishu.* 2nd ed. Taipei: Hanguang wenhua, 1991.

Wang Bomin. *Gudai xiaoxingyin xuanji.* N. p., 1979.

Wang Chi-ch'ien. "Yinzhang zai jianpie Zhongguo shuhua ti xiaoneng." *Dalu zazhi* 15, no. 2 (July 1957): 45-47.

Wang Chi-ch'ien, and Kathleen Yang. "The Mystery of The *Chang* Seal." *Ars Orientalis* 18 (1988): 151-60.

Wang, Fang-yu. *Introduction to Chinese Cursive Script.* New Haven: Far Eastern Publications, Yale University, 1958.

———. *Dancing Ink: Pictorial Calligraphy and Calligraphy Painting.* Short Hill: Wang Fangyu, 1984.

———. "The Seals of Ming Chip Fung." In *Fung Ming Chip*, 43-45. Hong Kong and New York: Hanart 2 Gallery, 1988.

Wang, Fang-yu, and Hsu Kai-yu. *Ch'i Pai-shih's Paintings.* Taipei: Art Book Co., 1979.

Wang, Fang-yu, and Richard Barnhart. *Master of the Lotus Garden: The Life and Art of Bada Shanren (1626-1705).* New Haven; Yale University Art Gallery, 1990.

Wang, Jing. *The Story of Stone: Intertextuality, Ancient Chinese Stone Lore, and the Stone Symbolism in "Dream of the Red Chamber," "Water Margin," and "The Journey to the West."* Durham and London: Duke University Press, 1992.

Wang Renshou, comp. *Jinshi dazidian.* 1926. Reprint. Taipei: Datong shuju, 1981.

Wang Shijie, ed. *Gugong minghua sanbaizhong.* Taichung: National Palace Museum and National Central Museum, 1959.

Wang Yuchi, ed. *Zhongguo shufa zhuanke xianshang cidian.* Beijing: Nungcun duwu chubanshe, 1989.

Wang Zhende and Li Tianxiu, eds. *Qi Baishi tanyilu.* Luoyang: Henan renmin chubanshe, 1984.

Wang, Zhongshu. *Han Civilization.* Translated by K. C. Chang et al. New Haven and London: Yale University Press, 1982.

Wang Zhuangwei. "Tan Daqian jushi suoyong yinzhang." In *Zhang Daqian jinian wenji*, edited by Ba Dong and Hong Chunxiu, 32-37. Taipei: National Museum of History, 1988.

Watson, Burton. *The Complete Works of Chuang Tzu.* New York: Columbia University Press, 1968.

Whitfield, Roderick. *Chinese Traditional Painting, 1886-1966: Five Modern Masters.* London: Royal Academy of Arts, 1982.

Wilhelm, Richard. *The I Ching, or Book of Changes.* Translated by Cary F. Baynes from the German version. New York: Pantheon Books, 1950.

Wilson, Marc F., and Kwan S. Wong. *Friends of Wen Chengming: A View from the Crawford Collection.* New York: China House Gallery, China Institute in America, 1975.

Winter, John, and Tamar Ellentuck. "The Photographic Enhancement of Seal Impressions." *Archives of Asian Art* 40 (1987): 74-77.

Wu Dongmai. *Wu Changshuo.* Shanghai: Renmin meishu chubanshe, 1963.

Xianggang zhongwen daxue wenwuguan cangyinji. Hong Kong: Art Gallery, Chinese University of Hong Kong, 1988.

Xiao Gaohong. "Yetan yinpu di qishi." *Xiling yiye*, no. 15 (July 1987): 32-33.

Xie, Zhiliu. "One of Badashanren's Cryptic Seals." *Orientations* 22, no. 2 (February 1991): 66.

Xiling yinshe, ed. *Yinxue luncong.* Hangzhou: Xiling yinshe, 1987.

Xu Shen. *Shuowen jiezi.* Beijing: Zhonghua shuju, 1963.

Yang Guangtai. *Qi Baishi tan zhuanke yishu.* Beijing: Shumu wenxian chubanshe, 1989.

Ye Erkuan. "Moyin chuandeng." In *Zhuankexue*. Vol. 27, pp. 131-172 of *Yishu congbian diyiji*, edited by Yang Jialuo. Taipei: Shijie shuju, 1986.

Ye Yiwei. *Zhuanke congtan*. Hangzhou: Xiling yinshe, 1985.

———. *Zhuanke congtan xuji*. Hangzhou: Xiling yinshe, 1987.

Yeh, Ch'iu-yuan. "The Lore of Chinese Seals." *T'ien Hsia Monthly* 10, no.1 (January 1940): 9-22.

Yokota Minoru. *Chūgoku impu kaidai*. Tokyo: Nigensha, 1976.

Yu Jianhua. *Chen Shizeng*. Shanghai: Renmin meishu chubanshe, 1981.

Zhang Yongming. *Zhuanshu yu zhuanshu bifa*. Beijing: Tiyu xueyuan chubanshe, 1987.

Zheng Jiaxiang. *Zhongguo gudai fobi fazhanshi*. Beijing: Sanlian shudian, 1958.

Zheng Xie. *Zheng Banqiao ji*. Hong Kong: Zhonghua shuju, 1979.

Zhonghua minguo qishibanian zhuanke zhanlan. Taichung: Taiwan Museum of Art, 1989.

Zhonghua wuqiannian wenwu jikan xiyinpian. Taipei: Zhonghua wuqiannian wenwu jikan bianji weiyuanhui, 1985.

Zhongguo meixueshi ziliao xuanbian. 2 vols. Beijing: Zhonghua shuju, 1980.

Zhongguo shuhuajia yinjian kuanshi. Beijing: Wenwu chubanshe, 1987.

Zhongguo meishu quanji. 60 vols. Beijing: Wenwu chubanshe and others, 1984.

Zhou Fagao, ed. *Jinwen gulin*. Hong Kong: Chinese University of Hong Kong Press, 1974-75.

Zhu Zhifan. *Zhuanfa tanyuan*. Preface dated 1911. Reprint, revised by Yang Jiaxiang. Taipei: Yiwen yinshuguan, 1971.

Zhu Xuchu. *Zhongguo gudai xianzhang shicui*. Nanjing: Jiangsu meishu chubanshe, 1987.

Zhuang Shen. *Zhongguo huashi yanjiu xuji*. Taipei: Zhengzhong shuju, 1972.

LIST OF CHINESE CHARACTERS

Aiji zhigou　愛己之鉤
Anji Wu Jun zhang　安吉吳俊章
Badashanren (1626-1705)　八大山人
baifurong　白芙蓉
Baishi weng　白石翁
baiwen　白文
Bancang　半倉
Bao Shichen (1775-1855)　包世臣
Baoyuantian　抱圓天
bei'e　碑額
Beiping Fangyu　北平方宇
beixue pai　碑學派
biankuan　邊款
Bichan　甓禪
Bingshang hongfei guan　冰上鴻飛舘
Cai Yong (A.D. 133-192)　蔡邕
Chang　長
Changle weiyang　長樂未央
changsheng wuji　長生無極
chanyita　蟬衣揚
Chen Hongshou (1768-1822; *zi* Mansheng)
　陳鴻壽，字曼生
Chen Jieqi (1813-1884)　陳介祺
Chen Lian (1730-1778)　陳鍊
Chen Shizeng (1915-1923)　陳師曾
Chen Yuzhong　陳豫鍾
Chijin Zhaoshi zhixi　赤鄞趙氏之璽
Chu Suiliang (596-658)　褚遂良
Chuqingjing yi yangzhi　處清靜以養志
Da jixiang　大吉祥
Dai Zude　戴祖德
Dasikong yinzhang　大司空印章

dazhuan　大篆
Deng Sanmu (1898-1963)　鄧散木
Deng Shiru (1743-1805)　鄧石如
Deshizhechang　得時者昌
Ding Jing (1695-1765)　丁敬
Dingsu　丁肅
Dong Qichang (1555-1636)　董其昌
Erjindietang yinpu　二金蝶堂印譜
Feihongtang yinpu　飛鴻堂印譜
fengni　封泥
Fofa sengbao　佛法僧寶
Fouweng　缶翁
Fubo jiangjun zhang　伏波將軍章
fugu　復古
Fusheng liuji　浮生六記
Gao Fu　高阜
Gaofeng　高鳳
Geng Jiazuo　耿嘉祚
Gouyouxu　鉤有鬚
Gu Congde (born ca. 1520)　顧從德
Gu Hao (active early 19th c.)　顧浩
Gu Xiang (active early 19th c.)　顧湘
guangeti　舘閣體
Gudao caotang　沽道草堂
Guiqulaici　歸去來辭
Guo Youdao　郭有道
Guquansou　古泉叟
guzhuo　古拙
Han Yu (768-824)　韓愈
hangqi　行氣
He Kongcai　賀孔才
He Shaoji (1799-1873)　何紹基

He Zhen (ca. 1530-ca. 1604)　何震
Hu Zhengyan (1584-1674)　胡正言
Huade ziran　畫得自然
Huaiyangwang xi　淮陽王璽
Huang Binhong (1864-1955)　黃賓虹
Huang Wenhan (active late 19th c.)　黃文瀚
Huang Wenhan shici changshou yin
　　黃文瀚詩詞長壽印
Huang Yi (1744-1802)　黃易
Huang Zhi Binhong　黃質賓虹
Huangshan shanzhongren　黃山山中人
Huangxiang　皇象
Huayulu　畫語錄
Hui　徽
Huzhou Anjixian　湖州安吉縣
Jia Sidao　賈似道
jiaguwen　甲骨文
Jian'nan Dongchuan jiedushi yin
　　劍南東川節度使印
Jiang Ren (1743-1795)　蔣仁
Jiehan moyuan　結翰墨緣
Jigu yinpu　集古印譜
Jijiu pian　急就篇
jijiuzhang　急就章
Jing guan　靜觀
jingjie　境界
Jingmingyuan bao　靜明園寶
Jinshixue　金石學
jinwen　金文
Jiushier weng　九十二翁
jixue　鷄血
jueju　絕句
Jungulu jinwen　攈古錄金文
Juran (active c. 960-980)　巨然
Kaimumiao shiqueming　開母廟石闕銘
kaozheng　攷證
Kaozhengxue　攷證學
Laigutang yinpu　賴古堂印譜
Li Shizhen (1518-1633)　李時珍

Li Tian siyin　李田私印
Li Yangbin (active 759-780?)　李陽冰
Li Zuoxian (d. 1876)　李佐賢
Liang Qingbiao (1620-1691)　梁清標
Liu Xian zhiyin　劉銑之印
liufa　六法
Liushi Baishi yin fuweng　六十白石印富翁
Liushi Baishi yin xuan　六十白石印軒
liuyao　六要
Lu Shihua (1714-1779)　陸時化
Luo Fuyi　羅福頤
Lüshi chunqiu　呂氏春秋
Mao Jin (1598-1659)　毛晉
mei　媚
Mei Qing (1623-1697)　梅清
Meihua shouduan　梅花手段
Meiyi yannian　美意延年
Mi Fu (1051-1107)　米芾
mian　面
miaozhuan　繆篆
miburongzhen　密不容鍼
mibutongfeng　密不通風
Mingyue dangtou　明月當頭
Mingyue qianshen　明月前身
Moyin chuandeng　摹印傳燈
Na Zhiliang　那志良
niaochongshu　鳥蟲書
Nidaoren　泥道人
nifeng　泥封
Ouyang Xiu (1007-1072)　歐陽修
Pan Tianshou (1897-1971)　潘天壽
Peijingtang　培荊堂
Puohe　破荷
qi　氣
Qi Baishi (1863-1957)　齊白石
Qi Baishi shoupi shisheng yinji　齊白石手批師生印集
Qian Dian (1741-1806)　錢坫
Qian Song (1807-1860; *zi* Shugai)　錢松，字叔蓋
Qiangnu jiangjun　強弩將軍

Qiangqigu 強其骨
Qiangyouer 墙有耳
Qiao Dazhuang (1892-1948) 喬大壯
qin 禽
Qingonggui 秦公簋
Qingtian 青田
qishouzhang 起首章
Qiu bei 丘貝
Qiushantu 秋山圖
Qizizhong 奇字鐘
Rixinchangji 日新長吉
ruyin yinni 如印印泥
ruzhui huasha 如錐畫沙
Sanshiwuju 三十五舉
Shanguoshan bei 禪國山碑
Shaoshi shiqueming 少室石闕銘
Shen Fu (1763-1808) 沈復
Shen Zhou (1427-1509) 沈周
shenhui 神會
shi 勢
shiguwen 石鼓文
Shiji zhilu 食鷄跖盧
Shijing 詩經
Shitao (1641-1710) 石濤
Shiyun shuhua 石韞書畫
Shizhong shanfang yinju 十鐘山房印舉
Shizhuzhai shuhuapu 十竹齋書畫譜
shou 熟
Shoujing 守靜
Shoushan 壽山
Shuhuashuoling 書畫說鈴
shukezouma 疏可走馬
Shuowen jiezi 說文解字
Shupu 書譜
Shuxiang mendi 書香門第
Shuyunlou yinpu 屬雲樓印譜
Sima wengzhi 司馬翁穉
Sisangongshan bei 祀三公山碑
Siyin 司印

Song ting 松庭
Soujin Qifeng dacaogao 搜盡奇峯打草稿
Soushiting 藪石亭
Su Shi (1037-1101) 蘇軾
Sun Guoting 孫過庭
Sun Xingyan (1753-1818) 孫星衍
tai 態
Taijitu 太極圖
Tang Xianzu (1550-1617) 湯顯祖
Tang Zuishi (1886-1969) 唐醉石
Tao Qian (365-427; *zi* Yuanming) 陶潛字淵明
tianbai 田白
Tianfa shenchenbei 天發神讖碑
tianhuang 田黃
Tianyuan jiangwu hubugui 田園將蕪胡不歸
Tianzhen 天眞
tiebi 鐵筆
tiexue 帖學
Wan 皖
Wang Beiyue (b. 1926) 王北岳
Wang Fu'an (1880-1960) 王福盦
Wang Mian (1287-1359) 王冕
Wang Qishu (1728-1800) 汪啟淑
Wang Qiu 王俅
Wang Shu (1668-1739) 王澍
Wang Zhiqi yin 汪之琪印
Wei shuai shan di baizhang 魏率善氏佰長
Wen Jia (1501-1583) 文嘉
Wen Peng (1498-1573) 文彭
Wen Shoucheng fu 文壽承父
Wen Zhengming (1470-1559) 文徵明
Wenqizhai tushuji 問奇齋圖書記
Wu Changshuo (1844-1927) 吳昌碩
Wu Dacheng (1835-1902) 吳大澂
Wu Junqing 吳俊卿
Wu Ling 吳泠
Wu Qi 吳奇
Wu Qiuyan (Wu Yan; 1272-1311) 吾丘衍, 吾衍
Wu Shifen (1796-1865) 吳式芬

Wu Xiansheng　吳先聲
Wu Xizai (1799-1870)　吳熙載
Wu Yi (1472-1519)　吳奕
Wu Yü zhiyin　吳育之印
Wu Yun (1811-1883)　吳雲
Wu Zhen (1280-1354)　吳鎮
wujinta　烏金搨
Wupiao shuhua　五瓢書畫
Wuya　吳押
Xi Gang (1746-1803)　奚岡
Xiang Yuanbian (1525-1590)　項元汴
Xiangsi dezhi　相思得志
Xiangxue zhai cang　香雪齋藏
Xianyang jiuke　咸陽舊客
xianzhang　閑章
Xiaojun　肖均
Xiaoshi shanfang yinpu　小石山房印譜
Xiaotang jigulu　嘯堂集古錄
xiaozhuan　小篆
Xibi langgan hupuolong　係臂琅玕虎魄龍
Xiling　西泠
xingcao　行草
xingshu　行書
Xinye cheng yin　新野丞印
Xiuhai　袖海
Xu Lin (1462-1538)　徐琳
Xu Sangeng (1806-1890)　徐三庚
Xu Shen (ca. 58-147)　許慎
Xu Shipu (1608-1685)　徐世溥
Xu Ziren shi　徐子仁氏
Xueran sanren　嚻然散人
Xueshantang yinpu　學山堂印譜
Xuexinting　學心聽
Xunyun　尋雲
yajiaozhang　押角章
yang　陽
Yang Shoujing (1839-1914)　楊守敬
Yang Xiong (53 B.C.-A.D. 18)　楊雄
Ye Erkuan　葉爾寬

Yihai　乙亥
Yijing　易經
yin　印
Yin Jing　印經
Yincun chuji　印存初集
yinpu　印譜
yinshouzhang　引首章
Yipiao　一瓢
Yizhu ciguan zhuren shouzhu　揖竹詞舘主人瘦竹
yuanzhuwen　圓朱文
Zhang Hao　張灝
zhangfa　章法
Zhao Mengfu (1254-1322)　趙孟頫
Zhao Shi (1875-1933; Guni)　趙石
Zhao Shuru (1874-1945; *ming* Shigang)　趙叔孺，名時棡
Zhao Zhichen (1781-1852; *zi* Cixian)　趙之琛，字次閑
Zhao Zhiqian (1829-1884)　趙之謙
Zhaowu jiangjun wushi sun Liang　昭武將軍五世孫亮
Zhe　浙
Zheng Xie (1693-1765)　鄭燮
Zhenhaijun jiedushi zhiyin　鎮海軍節度使之印
zhongfeng　中鋒
Zhou Bin (active late 17th c.)　周彬
Zhou Gongjin　周公瑾
Zhou Lianggong (1612-1672)　周亮工
Zhou Rong　周容
Zhu Da, see Badashanren　朱耷　參見八大山人
Zhu Jian (active 1572-1620)　朱簡
Zhu Qizhan (1892-)　朱屺瞻
Zhuankexue　篆刻學
zhuanshu　篆書
Zhuanxue suozhu　篆學瑣著
zhuwen　朱文
Ziyuan　滋園
Zizhen　子貞
Zizi sunsun yongbaoyong　子子孫孫永寶用
Zuo Qiuming　左丘明
Zuozhuan　左傳

PICTURE CREDITS

Black and White Photography

Plate 10, 34	Photographs by Michael Agee, Yale University Art Gallery
5	© 1992, The Art Institute of Chicago. All Rights Reserved.
6, 7, 8, 9, 37, 57, 58, 59, 60	Photographs by John Blazejewski
13, 15, 17, 18, 19, 26, 27, 29, 30, 33, 38, 41, 42, 43, 44, 45, 46, 47, 48, 49, 61	Photographs by Thomas Feist
11, 12 (Fig. 2), 16, 20, 21, 22, 23, 50	Courtesy of the Field Museum of Natural History, Chicago
32, 35, 36, 39, 40	Photographs by Shin Hada
3	Photograph by Robert Hensleigh
1, 4, 24 (Fig. 3), 25, 52, 56,	Copyright © 1992 by The Metropolitan Museum of Art
2 (Fig. 1b)	Courtesy of the Arthur M. Sackler Gallery, Smithsonian Institution, Washington, D.C.
53, 54, 55	Photographs by Heidi Schulman
28	Courtesy of F. Randall and Judith G. Smith
2 (Fig. 1a)	Photograph by John Tsantes
62 (Fig. 5)	Courtesy of Wang Fang-yu and Sum Wai Wang
14, 31	Photographs by Patrick Young

Color Plates

2, 3, 4, 6	Photographs by Thomas Feist
9	Photograph by Shin Hada
5	Photograph by Schecter Lee
7	Copyright © 1992 by The Metropolitan Museum of Art
1	Photograph by Maggie Nimkin
8	Courtesy of F. Randall and Judith G. Smith

CHINA INSTITUTE IN AMERICA

OFFICERS

Clare Tweedy McMorris, Chair
John H.J. Guth, Vice Chair
Millie Chan, Vice Chair and Secretary
James A. Perkins, Treasurer

PRESIDENT

Charles P. Wang

BOARD OF TRUSTEES

Pei-yuan Chia
Morley L. Cho
Herbert J. Coyne
Sharon Crain
JoAnn S. Delafield
George Fan
Laurette Soong Feng
Wen C. Fong
Houghton Freeman
Robert L. Hoguet
T.C. Hsu
Richard L. King
Anthony T. Limpe
Henry Luce III
Elisabeth L. Moore
Austra Root, Ex-officio
Sophie Sa
Elizabeth Seitz
Phillips Talbot
Oscar L. Tang
Marsha L. Wagner
Marie-Hélène Weill
Wan-go H.C. Weng, President Emeritus
Von Sung Yang
Shyh-Jong Yue
C.T. Shen, Emeritus
Chi-ch'uan Wang, Emeritus

CHINA HOUSE GALLERY

J. May Lee, Director
Heidi Schulman, Registrar
Hai Weilan, Project Assistant

GALLERY COMMITTEE

Millie Chan, Co-chair
George Fan
Wen C. Fong
Polly Guth
James C.Y. Watt
Marie-Hélène Weill, Co-chair
Wan-go H.C. Weng

ART COMMITTEE

Annette Juliano, Chairperson
Richard Barnhart
Vito Giacalone
Joan Hartman-Goldsmith
Maxwell Hearn
Jean Mailey
Mary Gardner Neill
Valrae Reynolds
Mary M. Tanenbaum
Suzanne Valenstein
Marie-Hélène Weill
Allen Wardwell
Martie Young

ART ADVISORY COMMITTEE

Theresa Tse Bartholomew
Claudia Brown
James Cahill
Betty Ecke
Wai-kam Ho
Donald Jenkins
Thomas Lawton
Lucy Lim
Yutaka Mino
Alfreda Murck
John Seto
Clarence F. Shangraw
Alexander C. Soper
Henry Trubner
Steven Weintraub
Marc F. Wilson
Wu Tung

EXHIBITION CONSULTANTS

Carl Nardiello
Stoneledge, Inc.
LeMar Terry

CORPORATE CHAIRMAN'S COUNCIL

Bank Central Asia
Chamarac Properties, Inc.
Citibank, N.A.
Computer Associates
Corning Incorporated
Delson International Inc.
Donaldson, Lufkin & Jenrette
Grumman International, Inc.
Hang Lung Development Co., Ltd.
Health Insurance Plan of Greater New York
The Hongkong and Shanghai
    Banking Corporation, Limited

Johnson & Johnson International
Pfizer International Inc.
Real Evergreen International
Stemton Group, Inc.
Time Warner, Inc.
Wertheim Schroder & Co., Inc.

FOUNDATIONS

Asian Cultural Council
AT&T Foundation
Mary Livingston Griggs and
    Mary Griggs Burke Foundation
Herbert and Jeanine Coyne Foundation
The Dillon Fund
Armand G. Erpf Fund
Golden Family Foundation
Edna and Yu-Shan Han Charitable Foundation
George Frederick Jewett Foundation
Albert Kunstadter Family Foundation
Lee Foundation, Singapore
The Henry Luce Foundation, Inc.
New York City Department of Cultural Affairs
New York Community Trust
Republic of China Commission
    on Tibetan and Mongolian Affairs
The Starr Foundation
Taconic Foundation, Inc.
J.T. Tai & Co. Foundation, Inc.
United Way of New York City
Ho-Ching Yang Memorial Foundation

PATRONS

Mrs. C.Y. Chen
Pei-Yuan Chia
China Institute Women's Association
Mr. and Mrs. Morley L. Cho
Mr. and Mrs. C.W. Crain
John and Julia Curtis
Paul B. Day, Jr.
Mr. and Mrs. J. Dennis Delafield
Mr. and Mrs. Douglas Dillon
Lawrence Delson
Robert H. Ellsworth
Mr. and Mrs. George J. Fan
Mr. and Mrs. Ivan Y.T. Feng
Mr. and Mrs. Michael Feng
Carol Griffis
Mr. and Mrs. John H.J. Guth
Mr. and Mrs. Robert L. Hoguet
Tina Chen and Marvin Josephson
Angela and Richard L. King
James J. Lally
Marie C. Lee
Mr. and Mrs. Anthony T. Limpe
Mr. and Mrs. Kuo Win Liu
Ambassador and Mrs. Winston Lord
Mr. and Mrs. Henry Luce III
Mr. and Mrs. Kwong M.Y. Lum
Diana McIlvaine
Mr. and Mrs. Howard McMorris II
Mrs. Maurice T. Moore
Mr. and Mrs. Donald E. Newhouse
Mr. and Mrs. Thomas L. Pulling
Rotary Club of Chinatown, N.Y.
Mr. and Mrs. Richard J. Salisbury
Dr. and Mrs. Frederick Seitz
Mary M. and Charles J. Tanenbaum

Oscar L. Tang
Charles Tse
Mrs. Gordon B. Tweedy
Mr. and Mrs. Cheng Ching Wang
Mr. and Mrs. Chi-ch'uan Wang
Vera Wang
Dr. and Mrs. John C. Weber
Marie-Hélène and Guy A. Weill
Wan-go H.C. and Virginia D. Weng
Von Sung Yang
Mr. and Mrs. James Ying
Henry Yung

SPONSORS

Margaret E. Aldous
Mr. and Mrs. Henry H. Arnhold
Koko Beall
Frederick C. Chen
Fred H. Chen
Michael Chiang
China International Trust
    and Investment Corporation
Roderick G.W. Chu
Jo Ann Connell
Catherine G. Curran
Robert Dewey, Jr.
Eleanor Thomas Elliott
Mr. and Mrs. Moe Eichen
Alan E. Feen
Gabriele Geier
Mr. and Mrs. James Goodwin
Dr. David P.J. Hung
Mr. and Mrs. Roger Ip
Jack Josephson
H. Christopher Luce
Dr. Robert W. Lyons
Mr. and Mrs. Charles C. Matteson, Jr.
Sally A. Miller
Lillian S. Neisloss-Schloss
New York Chinese Businessmen's Association, Inc.
Nicholas Palevsky
Martha B. Pickering
Albert Ping
Meredith M. Prine
David Rockefeller
Mrs. Laurance S. Rockefeller
Mr. and Mrs. Peter L. Rosenberg
Hortense S. Sacks
Mr. and Mrs. Theodore P. Shen
Abel Sheng
Samuel Sheng
Elaine Smithline
Mrs. Frederick M. Stafford
Jerome Stein
Sunnex, Inc.
Ambassador and Mrs. Phillips Talbot
Patricia P. and Henry Tang
Kaity Tong
Mr. and Mrs. Michael Tong
Jeanette S. Wagner
Ann Hotung Walkovik
Mr. and Mrs. Ray Wu
Patricia M. Young
Shirley Young
Mr. and Mrs. Robert Youngman

EXHIBITION SPONSORS

WORD AS IMAGE: THE ART OF CHINESE SEAL ENGRAVING
is made possible through the generosity of

John R. and Julia B. Curtis
The Dillon Fund
Grumman International, Inc.
The Henry Luce Foundation
Mary Livingston Griggs and Mary Griggs Burke Foundation
The Starr Foundation

and with additional support from
The Flushing Savings Bank
Fulton Beverage Corporation
GBSUA Industry Promotion Fund
New York Chinese Businessmen's Association
Sunnex, Inc.